Mom, I Have a Problem

An Unraveled True Story of Depression, Suicide, Resilience, and Second Chances

Sophia Manarolis

AUTHORITY
PUBLISHING

Praise For "Mom, I Have a Problem"

"I WAS GOING TO download the first chapter and read it later today, but after taking a quick peek at the first couple of sentences, I found myself reading until the end of the chapter. Wow Sophia! The way you bring the reader along through a very dark moment in your life is gripping, gut-wrenching, raw, and, dare I say it, uncomfortable. And that's exactly what we all need to understand: the struggles of someone's battle with depression and suicide. Thank you for sharing your most vulnerable moments, and I look forward to reading the entire book. We all need to gain a better understanding of depression and how it can affect us and our loved ones. Getting your "inside view" of what it feels like when your mind is not "home" is something we ALL need to understand to break the mental health stigma and drive change. It's about time somebody wrote like this!"

—Lia Gribilas

"I was reading your story, and I was picturing you. I can't explain it. You usually imagine characters. I just... I can't find the words. I'm not going to lie, though; when I got to the part about your mom, now being a mother, I literally almost broke down. How helpless a parent feels when such a monster has taken over their child's mind, and you can't do anything. I know the story isn't just based on that, but it got me really choked up. The saying goes, 'I'm hoping my story touches at least one person.' I believe your story will hit many, and I'm happy you're around to tell it."

—Georgia Makrigiannis

"I was putting off reading Chapter 1, and I wasn't sure if I wanted to read it. In the end, I read every line with goosebumps all over my body and tears rolling down my face. So glad that dreadful day wasn't your last!!! So glad your angels were there for you!! God bless you!"

—Voula Karnezis

"Powerful. Raw. Real. No "filter". These are just some adjectives that come to mind when reading Chapter 1. I was truly blown away. I just couldn't put it down, it's like I was transported right there with you and had a much better understanding of that monster, that all-encompassing invisible demon that could infect someone's life and who's just as deadly as his cousin cancer! It takes a tremendous amount of courage and strength to unveil yourself like this so publicly. You are sincerely inspirational, and I have no doubt this will help so many people out there. Thank you from the bottom of my heart. #grateful"

—Theo Giovanis

"Wow, Sophia...just phenomenal! Chapter 1 is so well written and very detailed...bringing us along in your deepest thoughts. You got my attention and will get every reader's attention, no doubt. This book will help many! I cried...I felt your pain and that of your mom. I wish you nothing but continued success stories from now on. Thank you for continuing to raise awareness. I can't wait to read the rest of the book!!"

—Roula Vrentzos

"Riveting!!! Keeps you wanting to know more, to know your story, to understand how these demons work. The end narrative will be phenomenal and useful for many to comprehend and help others suffering from this illness!"

—Lemonia Strapatsas

"Your vulnerability is commendable, Sophia... Through it, I hope you are able to not only help others, shed some light, and bring even more awareness to this terrible monster but also find peace."

—Eleni Papakonstantinou

"I read Chapter 1, and oh my God, what can I say? Do I start with the physical effect it had on my body...mental or emotional? I felt every single word you wrote...My breaking point (when the tears began) was your mother. God bless you for being alive, for sharing your story, for your courage, and for everything."

—Irene S.

"Sophia, I read the first chapter of your book, and I must say you are such a remarkable woman. You talk about this demon in you that tried to make you hurt yourself, but you overcame it. I just wanted to read more and more of your book as I was reading chapter 1. And yes, I cried when reading what you were going through. Love you."

—Despina Bourdaras

"I just finished reading Chapter 1 and can't stop crying. I need time to register it all. This was raw and scary. You had told me about your episodes, but reading this made it all so real... I am still crying as I write this. Your book will help a lot of people."

—Penny Chatzinas

"I got a chance to read the first chapter. It flowed so well, and knowing you and your story, I couldn't stop reading. There was a reason you did not die that day. Your purpose in life is not over! Keep helping those in need who might be going through the same thing. There are many people who love you and care about you, including me."

—Helen Mentzelos

"Sophia, I just read the first chapter, and all I can say is WOW! I was right there with you, feeling every person's emotions. I have never attempted to take my life, but there have been times I felt like that would be an option to consider. Your book is so needed in the world. I am so glad there was an army of God's angels watching over you so you can bring this important message to a world that so needs it. I see you on talk shows, stages, and even schools sharing your message to encourage others and give them HOPE! You ROCK, my friend. I am so incredibly blessed to know you."

—Sandie Grindel

Mom, I Have A Problem is real, raw, and intense. Sophia holds nothing back as she candidly shares her honest, most vulnerable, and revealing truth about what it's really like living with depression. Sophia is bringing so much light into the world with this book. I believe this book will be a lighthouse for many people living with depression and for those who love them. Not only will it change how we look at depression and open our eyes, but it will also equip us with the tools we need to fight and win!"

—**Lindy Lewis**

"It's 3:16 pm, and I finally finished reading Sophia's book on the issue of how depression can be the nastiest, most brutal, and unforgiving of monsters. I legitimately had to stop reading it, given how blunt Sophia is, how she does not sugarcoat her personal experience battling it, and how it affected her family and her path in life. I needed time to process it all truly! Please take care of yourselves, folks, and seek help as I have on occasion. Mental health and physical health go hand in hand and must be balanced together in a holistic sense! My compliments to Sophia, to her candor, to her courage, and to giving all a means for a far better life filled with gratitude, emotional wealth, and kefi* above all else. #its316andimalive"

—**Nicholas Pidiktakis**

*Kefi** - Greek word with no direct translation into English. When asking Greek speakers what "kefi" means, they say that it means you are joyful, spirited, passionate, happy, and in general, that you love life.*

"As someone who has experienced severe depression, I deeply empathize with the author. Her book presents a somber narrative of depression, interspersed with advice and anecdotes. Reading it sent chills down my spine and resurfaced memories of being in a similar state. I wish I had this book during those times! If you are grappling with depression, don't ignore it! It starts subtly, resembling a bad mood with seemingly rational explanations, but soon, it overwhelms you, draining everything positive from your life. Wondering how someone with depression feels? Read this book! If you have it and need help overcoming it, read this book!"

—Ivan Zasekrechenov

"Reading about the thoughts and experiences of a person attempting suicide was both unsettling and enlightening for me. This book vividly portrays the story of an intelligent, ambitious, and empathetic individual who becomes deeply entangled in the grip of depression to the extent that her actions spiral beyond the realm of sanity. It is a must-read for everyone, especially parents seeking insights into depression, suicide prevention, and compassionate approaches when dealing with someone grappling with this monster. I am truly impressed by Sophia's courage in candidly sharing her story, bringing this delicate and crucial topic into the spotlight for an open and honest discussion."

—Talha Shaikh

"As someone who has suffered from Major Depressive Disorder, Anxiety, and suicidal thoughts in the past, I relate deeply to this book. This is a raw and real view of depression that allows the reader to understand what this monster looks and feels like thoroughly. This book will guide anyone to a better understanding of depression and how to help a loved one suffering. I am so grateful that the author failed at her attempts to end her life; she turned her pain into purpose and is helping millions of people across the globe live better lives through her story of triumph and having founded the **3:16 Movement!**"

—**Tara LaFon Gooch**

Paperback ISBN: 979-8-9897577-2-5

Published by: Authority Publishing

www.authority-publishing.com

Printed in the United States of America.

Disclaimer

THIS BOOK IS CERTAINLY not for the faint-hearted, and it's filled with triggers! The content of **Mom, I Have A Problem** is for informational purposes only and is not intended to diagnose, treat, or cure any condition or disease. This is a vivid, raw, and unfiltered recounting of my personal experiences with depression, including some graphic details about some of my attempts to end my own life.

If you're on the verge of suicide like I've been, my hope is that this book will convince you that your life matters.

If you're in the middle of a suicide crisis, put this book down for now, do a Google search on the suicide crisis helpline of your country, and call them STAT...because YOU MATTER!

If your country is not listed anywhere on Google, please contact your local emergency services, or reach out to someone you love to help you do so!

REMEMBER: Your Life MATTERS!!!

This Book Is For You If:

• You are someone who appreciates authentic and inspiring stories, seeking narratives that capture the resilience of the human spirit amid life's challenges.

• You are someone looking for a powerful and emotionally impactful story that sheds light on the realities of depression.

• You are someone who doesn't have any form of depression yet seeks to understand and is willing to listen.

• You are a parent who wants to proactively educate yourself about depression, seeking guidance on early signs and strategies to support your child's mental health.

• You are a parent looking to better understand the impact of depression on family dynamics and gain insights into supporting a child or loved one through their struggles.

• You are a loved one who genuinely cares deeply for someone suffering from depression and seeks to understand how to support them through it.

• You are someone living with guilt or regret from the loss of a loved one to depression or suicide and are seeking some clarity.

• You are someone who may currently be living with depression and needs a little (or a lot) of encouragement and hope.

• You are someone who has personally experienced depression, anxiety, or suicidal thoughts, seeking a relatable and insightful perspective on these challenges.

• You are a caregiver, therapist, or counselor looking for personal stories to deepen your empathy of clients coping with depression so as to better serve and connect with them.

• You are an educator or school professional who aims to foster a compassionate and informed environment for students with mental health issues.

• You are a human being wanting to contribute to something greater than yourself by normalizing the conversation around depression and saving more precious lives.

HELP BRING H.O.P.E. TO humanity through the

3:16 Movement!

Let's **Help Open People's Eyes!**

Contents

This book is dedicated to those who have been there during the major depressive episodes that took over my life, especially those who stuck around and never gave up on me. You know who you are. I am eternally grateful to you.

To the fifty of you who preordered my book while I was writing it, I am forever grateful for the encouragement your gesture provided. Writing this book was no small feat, as a lot of unhealed trauma was unearthed. The good news is—GREAT news, actually—I did some next-level healing during and ever since this process, and I'm very much looking forward to writing Part 2!

To anyone else who has purchased this book ever since its release, THANK YOU for helping me grow the **3:16 Movement** and normalizing the conversation surrounding burnout, depression, and suicide.

With much love,

Sophia

"Alone we can do so little; together we can do so much." — Helen Keller

Prologue

THERE'S ALWAYS H.O.P.E.

After four major depressive episodes and a few suicide attempts, my life's purpose has been and continues to be to Help Open People's Eyes about their own mental health and the potential for it to go to shit because... guess what?

Depression DOESN'T Discriminate.

It can happen to every person reading this book right now, no matter your gender, age, sex, race, class, religion, ethnicity, ability, language, sexual orientation, or relationship status. Essentially, it can happen to anyone on the planet—including **you.**

Take it from me ... I was once a first-year university student with no history of depression or suicidal ideation (in myself or my family), just a history of applying *way* too much pressure on myself to succeed—something that today I call unnecessary suffering.

That year, at age eighteen, I had the first of many major depressive episodes. It lasted six months. It was debilitating enough for me to have to pause and withdraw from my studies midway through my first semester after having busted my butt to ace those midterms. This was the first time I had ever experienced such mental torment and the first time thoughts of self-harm had ever entered my mind.

Here's the thing most people don't know: If you have lived with major depression, you become susceptible to experiencing it again—a fact I seemed to have skipped over when studying for my psychology-related midterms and something that is not talked about in our society.[1]

So, six and a half years after recovering from major depression, just before entering the last semester of my master's program, it happened again.

And guess what? I recovered from that episode six months later. Six months after returning to university to complete my master's, it happened AGAIN! This time, though, things got a lot scarier, and on March 16, 2011, I tried to die.

I repeat:

Depression DOESN'T Discriminate.

Anyone, no matter how successful they may seem, *can* be affected!

---

1. https://www.ncbi.nlm.nih.gov/pmc/articles/PMC2169519/

Many who have considered suicide didn't want to die; they simply wanted the pain to stop. Suicide, though, is **not** the answer. Getting the right help *is*.

The day I tried to die will never escape my mind and has officially become the most important day of my life ... what I now call *3:16 Day* (third month, sixteenth day). It is the day I was given a second chance to live—to stick around and appreciate one of the greatest gifts I have ever been given: LIFE.

Somewhere along the way, I fell back into the trap of living as an immortal, and six years after recovering from that near-death experience, a lack of self-love and proper self-care led me into the worst major depressive episode yet. That thirteen-month period, which nearly killed me more times than I can count on my fingers, began one month after returning from my beautiful honeymoon. It led me to shut down the private practice I had worked hard to build over the years. Again:

Depression DOESN'T Discriminate.

Anyone and everyone, no matter how happy they have been and how many major positive life transitions they've walked through, can be affected.

As Tony Robbins, a well-known life coach I truly admire, has said at many of his transformative events, "If you can find grace within yourself from your worst experience, then maybe your worst experience has become your best." I know that's the case for me as

I have managed to transform my struggles with mental illness and attempted suicide into a Movement of gratitude and H.O.P.E — the **3:16 Movement!**

#its316andimalive, www.join316.com

Mom, I Have a Problem is an updated version of my first book, ***Depression Doesn't Discriminate***. With the previous title, it was wrongfully assumed that this book was solely for people currently suffering from depression when, in reality, it's a story about what it is like to live with this monster known as depression, which can open anyone's and everyone's eyes. You'll learn what can go through the mind of someone attempting to end their own life and how you can help someone you love suffering from depression.

As you journey through my experiences, it's crucial to understand the transformative power of language. A couple of months after completing the first version of this book, in January 2023, I engaged in a virtual coffee chat with an extraordinary mindset coach I connected with on LinkedIn (you can find more about this coach in the list of resources discussed in the Epilogue). As I recounted my story to him, I noticed that I repeatedly referred to myself as a "major depression and suicide attempt survivor," emphasizing the identity of "I AM" one and portraying "my depressive episodes," "my depression," or "my suicide attempts" as not only harsh but essentially—mine.

He questioned whether I was still experiencing depression and suicidal thoughts, prompting me to declare, "Hell NO" emphatically! However, he pressed further, asking if I was certain of this because my continued use of possessive language, such as "my," suggested that I still claimed ownership of depression and suicide attempts. Talking in the present tense about surviving through them implied an ongoing struggle. Was this truly the message I intended to convey to my subconscious mind and to my readers, followers, supporters, and anyone else I aimed to inspire with hope?

Honestly, I found myself suddenly speechless and mind-blown all in one. While I often spoke about the power of language and how certain words can detrimentally affect our self-esteem, self-confidence, and overall mental health, I had never realized that describing my experiences this way was the opposite of my intended message. It was contributing to my unnecessary suffering. I no longer claim ownership of those four major depressive episodes, and I am no longer surviving through suicide. Altering my choice of words has made an immense difference in how I share my story and discuss these challenging life experiences. I now encourage you to pay close attention to what you may inadvertently be hanging onto, which ultimately no longer belongs to you.

Because this book serves as an exact recording of the thoughts I had during several major depressive episodes, some verbiage used contradicts inclusive, person-first language. While I have reported here that the *monster* in my head used the word "retarded," it is not a word I condone. It is often used as a derogatory term to insult and demean individuals with intellectual or developmental disabilities, and I do NOT approve of this type of language or its harmful effects. Suppose this word is something you continue to use today. In that case, I kindly ask that you join many of us in spreading kindness and understanding, creating a more inclusive and respectful world for all, and substituting it with "a person with an intellectual disability."

Lastly, as you read through my book, you'll observe that when I refer to a specific center I frequented in Canada, the word 'center' is spelled the British English way, as that's the Canadian convention. However, I maintain consistency with the American English spelling when referring to centers without a specific title for the rest of the book.

Hopefully, this book will inspire you to take better care of your mental health.

"Your mental health is everything—prioritize it. Make the time like your life depends on it, because it does." — Mel Robbins

Chapter One
You'll Never Understand Me

WEDNESDAY, MARCH 16, 2011

(3/16/2011)

"Meet me at the store at noon. We're going to see Dr. Farquhar today."

Here we go. Another message from my brother. There's no way that's going to happen. I've done this before—I've been here before.

Anxiety flared through my body like fire.

Dr. Farquhar is great, but I saw him during the last episode. I can't do that again. There is no way I am going back to a psych ward. I'd rather die than go back there. I am done. This kind of life is simply not worth living. Today is the day I put an end to all this suffering.

I slowly rose from my best friend Olga's bed, grabbed my purse, and looked to ensure the bottle of Tylenol and a pack of Gravol I'd purchased a couple of days ago were there.

It's too bad Olga's at work. I would love to hug her one last time ... and say goodbye.

I saw Dr. Farquhar, a psychiatrist at the Douglas Mental Health Hospital, during a second major depressive episode. At that time, the *monster* known as depression had me convinced that I was mildly intellectually disabled. That's right, I—the person who had officially completed her master's degree in counseling at the University of Ottawa—strongly believed I was mildly intellectually disabled.

According to many psychiatrists I had spoken to, this was impossible. No matter how much I tried to convince them of how badly I suffered from mental challenges, they were adamant that an intellectual disability was impossible because not only had I made it into a graduate program, but I'd aced all my graduate work.

Yet after several trips to the psychiatric emergency room and having completed an eight-week outpatient program, I was convinced my intellectual disability wasn't being recognized, and I'd had enough of being misunderstood.

I am mentally retarded,[1] *not mentally ill. Everyone at the Douglas is mentally ill, so I don't belong with them there. There's no f*ckin' way I'm going back.*

I've got to find a place to disappear to. A place where I can swallow these pills and not be found while they take time to kick in.

Hmmmmm ... Where do I go?

---

1. See prologue

My brother's expecting me at the store, though. F*ck.

I left Olga's apartment with no idea what would happen next. I was so anxious that my body felt like it was burning. My thoughts were racing and irrational. I messaged my brother Tony.

"I'm on my way, but I don't want to return to the Douglas. Please don't take me there. Please."

"We'll discuss this when you get here. Just get here for noon."

Olga lived about twenty minutes from my parents' Park Avenue and Bernard Street store. That short drive was excruciating. I screamed, hyperventilated, and wept intensely. Anxiety had gotten the best of me.

I was so afraid of what I had decided to do. Did I really want to die? Did I? I still wasn't sure.

In retrospect, it's easier to say that I no longer wanted to live this way. I wanted the mental torment to end. But at that moment, the *monster* had definitely convinced me that putting an end to my own life was not only the best solution—it was the ONLY solution.

The goal was absolutely to die that day.

So off I went, toward my parents' store, turning onto streets that wouldn't directly lead me there. I went through my old neighborhood and considered parking in my relatives' driveway. I knew they were in Dubai and wouldn't be back in town for at least three months. There was no chance anyone would pass by their home on that day or at least a couple of days that followed, which is all I would need to ensure I made this work.

So I pulled in.

But how will this make them feel—knowing I ended my life while parked at their home?

Will this cause any trauma?

Is that fair to them?

Is that how I want them to remember me? As selfish, not considering how it would make them feel to have something like this associated with their home?

F*ck it. Find somewhere else in Outremont to do this.

The twenty minutes my brother had given me had passed, and he texted, asking me where I was. I ignored the texts, driving in circles not too far from him ... trying to find that special spot where I could park my car and go unnoticed for some time.

He proceeded to call. I flushed the call and, within minutes, shut off my phone. As I drove up and down Mont-Royal, Tony called 911 to file a missing person's report, even though I hadn't gone missing... yet. He begged and pleaded with the police to start the process because he knew I was suicidal—a major reason he wanted me to see Dr. Farquhar at noon.

Fortunately for all of us, the police took my brother seriously and filed a report. My brother then called my family and friends, even those across the border, in case I had driven into New York State and contacted them. Part of Tony was hanging on to the idea that I only wanted to get away from him and be left alone for a little while.

I continued to drive, thoughts racing a million miles an hour.

Am I allowed to park here? Will a meter attendant approach my car? I'm not sure how long it will take for this bottle of Tylenol to kick in. It could take hours before my organs stop functioning. I gotta make sure I don't get interrupted …

Is this a side of the street where the snow removal crew will pass? What is today? Wednesday? Do they clean the snow on the right or the left side of the Plateau? It's on the right side. I should be good here.

Are my back windows tinted enough so I won't get spotted? Is this park for children or pet owners? It's too cold for anyone to go to the park today, anyway! I think I'm good. I'm going to park my truck and make sure no one notices me getting into my back seat.

My anxiety had reached new heights, and because I'd read about suicide several times in the last couple of days, I knew that people tended to back down when the time came to swallow all those pills. I used whatever techniques I had to pump myself up to get something done. And, of course, the *monster* didn't hesitate to assist in the process.

You got this, Sophs. You got this.

You got this!

You can do this! Yes, you can!

This is for the best! You will no longer be a burden.

No one will have to deal with or take care of you anymore! You have to do this.

You have to!

For their sake and yours.

Do it.

Just do it!

One by one.

Let's go!

One more!

Don't stop.

Keep going.

One more.

Just keep swallowing!

This has to be done.

It's for the best.

Keep going!

One more.

You got this.

You can do this.

Almost there.

Just a couple more!

You got this!

You did it!

Where's the Gravol?

Take the Gravol now!

After swallowing fifty extra-strength Tylenol at warp speed, I took several Gravol, a doctor-recommended treatment for nausea and vomiting, to ensure I did not throw up all that I had just ingested.

Then I waited.

I waited to die, hoping it wouldn't be a slow and painful death.

I had read on suicide-related forums (yes, those exist) that once one major organ shuts down, it isn't long before the rest follow.

The *monster* really wanted me to die. As such, it mentally prepared me to do whatever it took to do so. Within about a half hour, I started feeling numb. I hadn't eaten anything in over twenty-four hours, and my empty stomach was absolutely not able to hold down all those pills.

So I threw up.

While staring at the floor in the back seat of my Ford Escape, I wondered,

What does this mean?

Will it still work?

Did I puke it all out?

Could there be any left in my system?

F*ck!

What do I do now?

I hope there is still enough in my system.

I was too numb to move, and I was prepared to wait. So I did, for nearly eight hours. At some point, about five to six hours in, I thought,

Am I dying yet?

Is it finally happening?

How much longer?

Is this all I'm going to feel? Or will it hurt more?

How will I know I'm really dying?

Not exactly the type of inner conversation the average person has on a Monday afternoon, yet there I was, having that exact inner conversation.

At some point, I woke up feeling relatively normal and told myself to call it a day. Clearly, this wasn't working. There was no point in sticking around in the back seat of an SUV in the middle of winter when my life was obviously not going to end at that moment.

Here's the thing: What may have happened outside my car all that time hadn't crossed my mind. It was as if the world had stopped. Anxiety had consumed me, and all that existed was what I could see in front of me.

It never occurred to me that my brother had contacted most of my good friends and family or that police officers were actively searching for a silver 2010 Ford Escape. Or that my aunts had gathered at my parent's house to be by my mother's side while she was losing her mind.

Neither had it occurred to me that, ironically enough, if this didn't work, I was going to wind up exactly where I hoped to avoid—the psych ward.

*F*ck it.*

I won't die today, so there's no longer a point in sticking around here.

Might as well call Tony and let him know I'm coming home.

As if nothing had happened, I opened my phone to call my brother and find out where he was. My Blackberry started ringing off the hook as soon as I opened it. The first call I saw coming in was from my cousin Perry. He usually texts me more than he calls, so I was taken aback when I saw his name on my call display. I ignored it because I only wanted to talk to my brother. As soon as I hit ignore, another call came, and another, and another. Next, text message notifications flooded in. My phone was going berserk.

Finally, I was able to call my brother. With a frightened voice, Tony answered and yelled, "YOU'RE ALIVE! Oh, thank GOD! WHERE ARE YOU?! WHERE ARE YOU? Are you OK? WHERE THE HELL ARE YOU?!"

The gravity of the situation finally began to set in. I did what I could to reassure him I was OK, but I couldn't tell him exactly where I was because several hours ago when I was anxious beyond measure, my brain hadn't registered what street I had turned onto. I finished telling him I was OK and got out of the car to figure out my location, but my legs didn't want to follow. They felt very heavy, and I almost fell. I had to hold my legs from just above my knee and lift them one by one to walk to the end of the street. What normally would have been a one-minute walk took a lot longer.

While I was on the phone, slowly and dreadfully making my way to the street corner, I heard my brother talking to someone else on another phone and my mom crying very loudly. That's what really drove home the gravity of the situation.

After telling my brother where I was, the walk back to the car wasn't as bad. Just as I entered the car, before I could even close my door, a police cruiser arrived.

The next morning, I found out that this was the same police officer who had rushed over to my parents' store to file a missing person's report for me. Seven hours or so after that, he was just about to go off duty when he heard through dispatch that the Ford Escape they were looking for was on St. Dominique, near Marie-Anne. He took the call and practically flew over to me.

The officer quickly checked to see if I was injured. I told him I was OK because I had thrown up. He grabbed my bottle of Tylenol and reported to the incoming ambulance how much I had taken, as well as his observations of how much had been regurgitated in the back seat.

Before I knew it, the ambulance, Tony, and my mother had arrived.

While crying hysterically, my mom pushed through everyone and hugged me, yelling in Greek, "Why would you do such a thing? We all love you. Why would you do this? What did we do to you?"

My brother was also crying, but before he could approach me, the paramedic asked that everyone step aside so I could be taken to the emergency room. And then the judgment really began.

As I lay there in the ambulance, the paramedic told me that I shouldn't have done this—that I had made a lot of people suffer today and that there's always another solution.

Having little energy to say much, tears rolling down my cheeks, I said, "You'll never understand me."

Chapter Two
"Mom, I Have A Problem"

HERE'S THE THING WITH major depression—if you've had one episode, you automatically become more susceptible to another during periods of great distress.

I was once a first-year university student with **no** history of depression and suicide in my family whatsoever, just a history of applying way too much pressure on myself to succeed, something that today I call UNNECESSARY SUFFERING. At age eighteen, I had the first major depressive episode, and it lasted six months. It was debilitating enough for me to have to withdraw from my studies midway through my first semester—after having worked really hard to do well on my midterms, with learning disabilities and all.

In late October 2002, not long after completing midterms for my first semester majoring in political science at McGill University, I experienced an anxiety attack at the library after realizing that my final exams were going to be cumulative. This meant I would be tested on all the material I had already studied for the midterms and all the material that followed the midterms.

The problem was that, due to my learning disabilities, whatever I had managed to memorize up until that point was as good as gone. I knew

I wouldn't be able to learn new material on top of learning the old material all over again, so I began to feel helpless and hopeless.

My high school experience wasn't the greatest. I had teachers who truly didn't care, some who looked like they had better things to do with their time, and some who simply never should have been allowed to teach. And yes, this is one of those times when the word "should" is very much appropriate (more on this later in the book).

By the time I hit grade 11, I was dead set on becoming a lawyer. But let's be real, I was pretty clueless about law back then. I just heard my dad over the years say his daughter was going to be a lawyer, and hence, I went with that. Because of this path, I had "chosen," I opted out of being in classes with science stream students. As a result, they put me in classes with the "dumb students," which is how the teachers referred to those of us who couldn't make it to science. When one of us asked our math teacher to clarify something he had just taught, he stared at us condescendingly and, in French, said:

"You will be singing in subway stations."

We could cheat on tests and get away with it. Hence, my learning disabilities went unnoticed throughout my entire high school education. It didn't help that my parents were immigrant workaholics who knew nothing about what high school work entailed and how I was getting by. They had no idea that their daughter would have likely never finished high school if not for the cheating she had to do.

Given my experience, I can't stress enough the importance of carefully choosing a school for your child's secondary education. Those years are an important and formative period in a person's life and can significantly affect their future. They may form friendships that last a lifetime and meet mentors who guide their career paths—or they may have the kind of teachers I did who very much contributed to lowering my self-esteem, self-worth, and self-confidence. Please choose wisely.

Before university, I studied for two extremely challenging years at Marianopolis College. It would take me ten hours of study to get through a single chapter of my textbooks. I didn't have much life outside of school and didn't do all the fun "transitionary" activities that most students do as they grow from teens to adults. The library became a second home where I felt comfortable.

Meanwhile, my family, for the most part, believed I was either a "nerd" or a very dedicated student doing everything I could to get into McGill and that spending so much time studying was normal. But nothing was normal about spending that much time in the books when I hadn't reached university level yet.

For those living outside of Quebec, the first year of this college program is the equivalent of grade twelve in the US, and the second year is the equivalent of freshman year (first year) in university.

After countless hours in the library, I completed the Marianopolis College program in two years, made the Dean's List for three semesters, and got accepted into McGill University. My goal had been to enter the law program, but I was told that it was best to first do a bachelor's degree in a program like political science to be better prepared to take on a law degree.

I had applied to two other universities in Montreal, Concordia and U of Montreal, but to make Poppa Manarolis proud, I had to choose the more widely known McGill. But the truth is, Poppa M. never had a single clue about what it takes to complete these programs, how McGill is not the only answer, and how, toward the end of my last semester, while trying to complete a project for my marketing class, I'd had a severe and debilitating anxiety attack.

My mom witnessed it as she momentarily came upstairs from their restaurant to check on my grandmother in our living quarters above. I cried and cried and told her that if I failed this project, I would not get into McGill, and if I didn't get into McGill, I wouldn't become a lawyer. If I didn't become a lawyer, my life was over—yes—over.

The pressure was real, yet my family had no idea. Even though my mom was witnessing the side effects of this pressure, she didn't know what to do. She tried to calm me and tell me my life wouldn't be over, but the conversation didn't open my eyes to other possibilities because she had to run back down to the restaurant for the supper rush.

I eventually calmed down, and when of sound mind, I reached out to my teammates to figure out something else for our group project.

Finally, we were able to submit it and receive a passing grade. My Marianopolis days were then officially over, and my McGill ones would begin after the summer of 2002 had ended.

When I started university in September, I soon realized that being at McGill would not be a cup of tea. Five classes at McGill were certainly NOT the equivalent of eight at Marianopolis College. The McGill program at large was demanding, and boy, could it ever be taxing on someone who never really cared about political science, to begin with.

You would think I would've had a clue after graduating from Marianopolis College that since the classes I loved the most were psychology-related, I would major in psychology, but no. The path was clear: law was my future, and political science was the most recommended way to get there.

So, there I was, pressuring myself to get through all this uninteresting material. I had no study strategies, no concept of self-care, no knowledge of what minimal sleep while applying this much pressure could do to my brain, and no idea yet of the nightmare that awaited me.

By the time I had that 2002 panic attack in the library, I had just read the course curriculum for one of my courses. I discovered that for my Introduction to International Relations class, the final exam was going to be cumulative. This threw me off tremendously. I had to read that part again, verify with another student in the class that I understood correctly, and then sit with myself and figure out how on earth I would pull that off. The mere idea of restudying all the material I had just regurgitated for the midterm, on top of all the material we had to learn in the six months that followed, made me very uneasy.

I decided to distract myself and instead moved on to study for another class. When I began reading through that class's course syllabus, dread settled into my stomach. I quickly shuffled through all my folders, looking for the other syllabi, and soon realized that ALL my final exams would be cumulative.

Within moments, I began hyperventilating.

My body was very much sent into a state of fight-or-flight. This was certainly the most intense anxiety I had ever experienced, and the feeling wouldn't go away. I began to cry and ran out of the library where I could cry really loud and not disturb others. I sobbed, choked over my saliva in the process, and eventually threw up in a corner of the campus grounds.

This was a destabilizing and frightening experience, as I had never lost control of my mind and body like that before. I returned to the library, packed up my stuff, and headed to my next class, where I could not concentrate. All I could do was obsess over what I had just learned about my finals and what I could do to get out of them.

But there was no getting out of it. I was no longer in high school, where cheat sheets would save the day. I was no longer able to get tests in advance. I could no longer get help from my brother the way I had before. Cheating at McGill was a serious academic offense that frightened me intensely. The mere idea of getting caught contributed to my anxiety because I thought that without going to McGill and becoming a lawyer, my life would be over.

As I continued to focus on variables I could not control, feelings of helplessness arose. This is why I offer tools today to help people shift their focus to what they **CAN** control; that is a lot more empowering. Alas, I did not know then what I know and teach now.

Additional depressive symptoms crept up, and in no time, it was blatantly obvious that I had a serious problem.

I no longer slept well or enough. I was no longer interested in attending activities I once enjoyed, such as dance practice. I cried in the shower and anywhere, really. I ate less and less and constantly feared what tomorrow would bring. These symptoms persisted well over two weeks. One day, I broke down while consulting my psychology textbook from Marianopolis College when I confirmed that I was indeed experiencing depression.

My mom was coming upstairs from the restaurant and noticed what was happening. She immediately tried to run to my rescue, but the conversation went south shortly after sharing what was happening and what I believed would be best for me.

"What's wrong, Sophie? What happened? Why are you crying?"

"Mom, I have a problem ..."

"What do you mean?"

"Mom ... I really can't do this anymore."

"Do what?"

"I can't study anymore. I can't go to class anymore."

With her tone slightly more elevated, as if the blood had already rushed to her head, she said, "What do you mean? Today? Or at all?"

"This semester. I can't finish this semester. I have a problem."

At this point, significantly angrier, she yelled at me, "Are you out of your mind? This can't be happening again! Your brother dropped out of university, and now you? You want to do the same to us?"

"Mom, you don't understand. Please let me read what it says here about what's going on with me. I have a problem."

While yanking me by the shoulder, she said, "The only problem you have is that we spoiled you too damn much! You don't care about anything or anyone. You don't even care about yourself. Look at you; you don't care about your appearance, how you dress, or how you carry yourself. You don't do any physical activity or anything to lose weight. You don't help out at the store when I need you anymore, you don't do any chores, you don't offer anything to this family really, and now you want to quit school too?"

"Go ahead. QUIT school. But if you think I am just going to let you sit here all day and not lift a finger, you have another thing coming. You don't want to go to school and do something with your life? Then you'll work day in and day out at the restaurant for the rest of your life. There's no way you'll do whatever you want with us and take advantage of us. NO WAY!"

"Mom ... please ... I have a problem."

Then, she walked away because the restaurant delivery line was ringing off the hook. We had an extra phone in our home connected to the restaurant for moments where she had to step away when perhaps the wait staff would be too busy to tend to the incoming calls. My parents definitely didn't have a clue about the concept of work-life balance, and frankly, as a result, for most of my life, up until maybe a couple of years ago, neither did I.

Mom wrote down the customer's order and rushed back to the store as the delivery lunch rush was soon to begin. Whatever she had intended to come upstairs to get at that point no longer mattered because, instead, she'd gotten the disappointment of her life.

Looking back, I understand how scared and helpless my mom felt underneath all that anger. Those are uncomfortable emotions that no one likes to feel, and as usual, anger stepped in to mask what was really happening. Feeling angry is much more comfortable than feeling whatever is usually beneath it. I have years of experience in providing anger management counseling and have developed more empathy for those who struggle with expressing their anger effectively. Lack of proper education on anger and communication is a contributing factor. I hope that one day, my course module on anger will be included in high school curricula worldwide.

Bottom line: I understand where my mom's reaction came from, and I continue to be grateful today for all her support and strength throughout these four major depressive episodes that occurred over a fifteen-year span. She is a genuine hero if you ask me, and my goal is to help her heal by writing my next book and future books and involving her in the writing process. I believe this will help her achieve the healing she deserves.

Needless to say, I continued to cry, now with more reason than I had before. All I could do was hope that my big brother would be more understanding and open to what I had to say. He was the person I felt the safest being myself with, as he was more present in my life growing up than my workaholic parents.

Eventually, my brother came home, and I shared my experience with him. I was not met with the same reaction but rather with mild confusion and an unknowingness of what to do. I told him that a teacher's assistant in one of my classes who saw me struggling suggested I visit the McGill Counselling Clinic and speak to an academic advisor about my options. So, my brother helped me with this. We made some calls, and meetings were arranged to see a counselor and the academic advisor of my faculty.

I went to the McGill Counselling Clinic for an intake session the next day. For those who don't know, an intake session is an initial appointment for the counselor to gather basic information about you and your background. You also learn more about the services available and any other referrals they would like to provide for external services that are highly recommended to complement your treatment plan.

Midway through the intake, the counselor, a graduate student in training, realized that I was likely going to require help beyond what was offered at the center. She also suggested that I speak to my academic advisor as soon as possible to determine the best course of action for my studies.

Shortly after my session, I contacted the academic advisor of my faculty, Paul Olioff, who told me he had a spot for me a little later that same day. Luckily, my brother had waited outside my counseling session and was willing to come with me to see the academic advisor, as I evidently had a hard time keeping it together and was pretty worried about what my future held at the university.

I've got to give it to Paul. As I write about this in 2022, I understand why he was recently awarded the 2022 Dean of Students Award for Excellence in Undergraduate Academic Advising. Students and colleagues nominated him for his helpfulness and empathy, among many other beautiful qualities. I can vouch that he truly deserves this award.

Twenty years ago, when I entered his office, he made me feel like I was the most important person to him at that moment. In his office, I didn't feel like I needed to be silent, and I didn't feel misunderstood. I was grateful for that, especially since meeting an academic advisor regarding pausing my studies at such a prestigious university could have gone the other way. In fact, if Paul hadn't been so empathetic and understanding, if he hadn't shown me that it was OK to withdraw temporarily from my studies for such a serious reason and that I would be welcomed back as soon as I recovered, I might not be here today.

The suicidal thinking had already begun; I was just too scared to voice it to anybody. Had I continued to push through my semester with such debilitating anxiety, among other major depressive symptoms, I may have jumped on the metro tracks back then as the thought had crossed my mind a couple of times on my way home from class. Paul, if ever you read this ... THANK YOU.

I followed the steps Paul suggested, such as seeing a doctor and writing an official letter to the dean of my faculty requesting withdrawal from the current semester. The best part, and I say this in the most sarcastic way possible, was when I visited my Greek family doctor. After I honestly answered his question about whether I had thoughts of suicide, he replied, "Don't do that. Only stupid people commit suicide."

My eyes still continue to roll so far back into my head when I think of that moment. If you're of Greek origin, I know you probably feel me.

The doctor referred me to a psychologist, but my father, known throughout the area as Johnny Buymore after the name of our family business, was having none of it. "There's no way MY daughter is going to a psychologist." Johnny Buymore's daughter could NOT be seen as "crazy," and going to a psychologist would mean just that. What would people think? What would people say? The way my parents saw it, I hadn't been deprived of anything growing up; how dare I make the family look bad? Again, if you're of Greek origin, I know you feel me and know that I feel you. So, I threw out the referral and never looked back.

I was left with a prescription for medication that I was too scared to take because I had read about nasty side effects and also heard American TV commercials at night enumerating all the side effects, including that taking said medication might lead to thoughts of suicide and suicide itself. Go figure—the very same thing that was supposed to help treat the depression could also make me want to die. Nope, definitely wasn't feeling it, so I tossed that paper in a drawer and carried on with the last of Paul's recommended steps, including writing my letter to the dean.

As I wrote the letter, I cried, yet I experienced relief, too, as the idea of not having to study for those final exams led to an immeasurable pressure being lifted from my body. Still, writing the letter continued to be difficult, and when I asked my brother to review it, tears rolled down *his* face as he couldn't believe what was happening to his little sister. He also not-so-secretly feared I wouldn't return to university after dropping this semester, as he did not return himself. His feelings of guilt were now also being projected onto me. I went from feeling relieved to experiencing the heaviness of guilt, all in a matter of thirty minutes.

But it had to be done. There was no way I was going to pull off a successful semester.

The next couple of months were far from pleasant. It was the first time in my life I had ever experienced such mental torment. Guilt is a major symptom of depression, and my self-worth was very much contingent upon doing well in school and making my parents proud.

That meant self-loathing was very quick to follow in the list of uncomfortable feelings I experienced. I had lost thirty pounds by this point and definitely would have benefited from a new wardrobe, but when you hate your life as much as I did, shopping for clothing is far from appealing. I also felt very guilty about "going nowhere with my life" and not working, so the idea of spending money on myself was out of the question.

Because we were in the middle of the Christmas season, my father insisted on giving me money to go shopping, and so a few days before Christmas, my brother and Mary, his girlfriend at the time and one of my best friends, took me shopping.

If you've ever wondered why buying things makes you happy, when you buy something, you get a little rush of dopamine, giving you a sense of control or happiness. Dopamine is an essential brain chemical that has a role in our ability to experience pleasure or pain.[1] It has been proven time and time again that a dopamine deficiency can cause symptoms associated with depression, as it drains the joy from life and can leave you feeling apathetic and hopeless, as was the case for me.

So when my father handed me money to go shopping, Tony and Mary momentarily hoped that the Sophie they knew was back, as my mood did shift quite a bit during that trip. I also really enjoyed buying gifts for friends and family, and hence, the quick surge of dopamine deceived Tony and Mary.

On the way home, I was still riding the high of shopping, but shortly after we walked into our house and I sat on our living room couch, my dopamine levels dropped along with the bags. It's as if the last few hours had never happened. My parents didn't get to experience what Tony and Mary had and had a hard time believing that the trip didn't do the trick. This may have very well been the first time in their lives when throwing money at a problem didn't actually fix it.

Within a couple of days, it was Christmas, and though I was dressed in some of the new clothing I had recently purchased and looked

---

1. https://news.umich.edu/pleasure-and-pain-study-shows-brain s-q-pleasure-chemicalq-is-involved-in-response-to-pain-too/

rather attractive physically, cracking a smile was nearly impossible. I found myself leaving the living room where the family was gathered and going to the room next door to sit alone at one end of the couch.

My mom, though busy hosting and doing her usual running around, aiming to please everyone at the party, managed to check on me. She sat beside me on the couch and, with sadness in her voice, started asking why I wouldn't come and spend time with my aunts, uncles, and cousins, whom she knew I loved so very much.

I turned to her with a hopeless look and said, "MOM... I have a problem."

And as a tear rolled down her face, "I know," she said.

Chapter Three

"I'm Really Scared, T. I Don't Wanna Die"

THE DAY AFTER CHRISTMAS, I walked up the street to my dad's meat market. When I entered the building, I noticed my parents and brother were in the office having what seemed like a pretty serious discussion. As I approached, I heard my dad telling my brother, "I don't care what you're in the middle of; drop everything and find your sister the best psychologist in the country."

My brother said he wasn't sure where to start but would contact a friend who worked at the Royal Victoria Hospital and ask him for help.

"I don't care what it costs. What the hell is the point of working this damn hard if I can't make my kid better? Don't return to the store until you find someone to help Sophie."

Within a day, I had an appointment set up with Dr. Pearl Rothenberg, a psychologist in Westmount. After conducting my intake, Dr. Rothenberg provided me with the local suicide helpline (Suicide Action Montreal) on a little piece of paper to carry with me in my wallet (keep in mind, this was 2002). She also said not to hesitate to call if my thoughts ever worsened in between sessions.

I will spare you the long details of what ensued during those six months of therapy, but I will mention that throughout our time together, Pearl sent me for multiple tests, including blood work, to determine how well my thyroid was functioning. She even had me tested for ADHD, as I had insisted from the very beginning that my issues with concentration and memory existed long before the major depressive episode. Turns out, I did, in fact, have hypothyroidism (underactive thyroid), a disease I am still treated for today. I also had ADHD, along with other learning disabilities, including an auditory processing disorder.

I remember sitting in the neuropsychologist's office a few days after he had conducted the assessment, listening to what he'd found, and I cried as he shared the results. He thought I might be relieved to find out, but at that point, I hated myself more for "officially" having something wrong with me. Oh, the power of labels.

By the summer of 2003, I had fully recovered. I could resume my studies in the fall term, this time majoring in psychology and with the proper and much-needed accommodations from the disability resource center at my university. I completed my BA in psychology, volunteered in the field, and started a master's in counseling psychology at the University of Ottawa in 2008. All was well with the world and my mental health—or so I thought.

As I mentioned earlier, if you have lived with major depression, you become susceptible to experiencing it again—something I seemed to have skipped over when studying for my psychology-related midterms and not a topic commonly talked about in society at large.

So, six and a half years after recovering from major depression and just before entering the last semester of my master's, it happened again.

How? How could this happen again? I didn't struggle during my master's anywhere near as much as I did studying for my bachelor's degree, so where was all this coming from?

I had just finished 2009, the most incredible year of my life to that point. My YES year—the year I completed two internships and, during the process, felt so fulfilled when counseling people. The year I fell in love again. The year I traveled to New York on numerous occasions, went to Boston and Toronto, and then Dubai for the first time (where I nearly broke my face while flying off an ATV out in the desert). The year I visited Greece *twice*, I met new people and made many new friends, some of whom are still in my life today. How could this happen after having lived THAT kind of year?

Turns out that sleep is important.

So is processing your emotions after a few consecutive losses.

And so is NOT obsessing over the idea of being depressed again.

What I mean by all this is that when saying yes to life, you still need to say yes to sleep. Instead, that year, I drove almost two hours to Montreal practically every weekend while studying and completing my internships in Ottawa. I abolished the possibility of resting after an intense week in my program. Sleep didn't matter much to me. But, in reality, sleep *really* matters.

Simply put, better sleep means no burnout! The better you sleep, the more you optimize your daily performance and productivity. A productive workday makes room for a stress-free evening wind down, but in 2009, I either studied or went out after class. Winding down wasn't an option in my mind.

Poor sleep can also create difficulties regulating emotions that, in turn, often leave one extra vulnerable to depression in the not-so-distant future.[1] This can happen to every single one of you reading this book, not just those who have already experienced depression. In my case, though, having lived through it already, running on fumes and poor sleep was a recipe for disaster. It continues to be for me today—which is why learning to say NO to things that don't positively contribute to my mental health has been paramount in my still being around to share this with you today.

As for processing my emotions, in 2009, I left myself no room to grieve after 2008 brought losses that included the end of a friendship, a four-year relationship, and losing my grandma and my dear uncle Nick—a person who supported me the most during the first depressive episode.

---

1. https://www.ncbi.nlm.nih.gov/pmc/articles/PMC7181893/

Between the loss of my uncle and the relationship, I had an extremely hard time during the holidays and jumped at any opportunity to get out of Montreal. That opportunity came at the end of 2008 when my best friend Olga said she wanted to go to Times Square to watch the ball drop.

I had never been apart from my family on New Year's Eve, and one may have argued that now wasn't the time to do so. Thankfully, I was not met with resistance from my mom, as she could see I had been through a lot and thought getting away might do me some good.

As Olga and I rode the bus to New York, I read up on the story behind the Times Square ball drop. Each year, thousands gather in Midtown to ring in the New Year. At 11:59 p.m., the Waterford Crystal and LED ball begins its descent, and all who have gathered unite to count down the final seconds of the present year and celebrate the beginning of a new year full of hope, challenges, changes, and dreams.

This made me even more excited to ring in the New Year with Olga. And that we did! It was a surreal experience to be in Times Square, dancing and singing our hearts out from 4:00 p.m. that day. One moment, we were listening to Lionel Richie live, and the next, the Jonas Brothers. They played for us every couple of hours until the time came for them to repeat their concert on live television for the millions watching all over the world.

In those last couple of minutes, I began to cry. During the countdown, I let all the tears flow. I don't think I'd ever felt so hopeful for a more promising new year ahead, and after the ball had officially dropped, it was as if all the weight of 2008 dropped off my shoulders along with it. Talk about instantly feeling *lighter, freer,* and more *alive.*

I decided right then that 2009 would be the best year of my life, and I wasn't going to let ANYTHING stop that. The problem, though, was that it was like I'd shut off a switch and blocked all that had happened. That night could have been the beginning of a very healthy healing process. Still, instead, it was an overnight mindset metamorphosis that didn't allow me to go through grief as naturally and honestly as possible.

Here's the thing: Grief inevitably happens when you lose something or someone important to you. If you suppress grief and all its associated emotions, you'll delay the healing process, see your feelings explode later, and/or live a very inauthentic life. When faced with loss, moving through grief with self-awareness and courage is important. You can also do this with the help of a counselor.

When I worked under contract with several employee assistance programs, I saw hundreds of clients a year, and at least a third of those who contacted the service did so because they had a hard time dealing with a loss or several losses over a short period. We typically saw each other for four to six sessions and worked on alleviating the distress they experienced through different stages of grief, though the intent was *not* to speed up its process.

By providing strategies and tools on how to better navigate their feelings of guilt and sadness, how to better cope with their anger, and how to reduce anxiety and improve sleep, I essentially helped my clients reduce, if not eliminate, the unnecessary part of the suffering they experienced. The bottom line is that you don't have to process grief on your own, and I highly recommend you don't.

While dealing with grief, often we want to speed through it, get it over with, and be done with it—but we need to honor it and give it our time and attention until it gradually loses strength. The thing is, what I know and teach now, and what I knew then, is completely different. That night in Times Square, I decided that 2009 would be the best year of my life, and I wouldn't let *anything* stop that. Meanwhile, I had recently experienced multiple stunning losses. Being able to make mindset shifts in life is important to move forward and grow, but there's a time and place for everything, and at that point, a very abrupt and intensive mindset shift was not the answer.

By ignoring my grief and need for sleep, I spent 2009 having the time of my life, which meant that no one expected what happened at the end of that marvelous year.

I felt burned out throughout November 2009. I was stressed and fatigued but pushed through it all to complete my second internship and second-to-last semester. If left untreated, though, burnout can become part of one's everyday life and eventually lead to anxiety and/or depression. There's truly a fine line between burnout and depression, and if one isn't careful, crossing to the dark side where the *monster* takes over is inevitable.

Burnout symptoms vary depending on which phase of burnout you're in. In general, symptoms may present as physical, emotional, or behavioral.

Physical symptoms include:

- feeling tired

- difficulty sleeping

- a change in appetite

- headaches or muscle pain

Emotional symptoms include:

- lacking motivation

- feelings of self-doubt

- failure or loneliness

- feelings of dissatisfaction

Behavioral symptoms include:

- social isolation

- not performing your responsibilities

- work-related anger outbursts

So here I was, in December 2009, back in Montreal, experiencing many of the above symptoms. Toward the middle of the month, I no longer wanted to leave my basement and didn't really care to see anyone. I clearly needed a break.

Christmas Day rolled around, and I'm pretty sure I was myself, but by Boxing Day and the following days, I was even more fatigued and did not want to do anything other than rot in front of my television. This did not sit well with my mom, and she felt very anxious upon seeing the similarities between what I'd experienced in December 2002 and what I was now experiencing in December 2009.

My mom was concerned more and more as the days went by, and she expressed to Olga her fears of my possibly being depressed again. About four days before New Year's Day of 2010, while watching TV in the basement, Olga suggested we get coffee with a friend. I said I wasn't in the mood, and Olga said, "Sophs ... Do you think you might be depressed?"

Stupefied, I asked, "What? Where the f*ck did that come from?"

"Well ... you haven't been yourself lately, and your mom is pretty sure you are going through what you did in your first year at McGill."

"What?"

"Babe ... I don't know; I didn't know you back then, so I'm not sure what she's talking about exactly, but she's too afraid to approach you with this and has been expressing her concerns to me quite a bit lately."

I was in shock. "No," I said, "there's no way I'm depressed again. No f*ckin' way!"

I paused momentarily and thought about what Olga had just said ... what my mom was thinking ..., and how I had been acting throughout December. Before I knew it, the blood rushed to my head, and an anxiety attack was upon me.

"No. This can't be happening ... not again ... No! I can't go through that again, Olga. No, she's wrong! There's no way!"

"Babe, calm down. I was just asking if you might be depressed; I'm not telling you that you are. Breathe. We can figure this out."

"Olga, you don't understand. I really can't go through that ever again. It was awful, just f*ckin' awful!"

"I hear you, but please calm down. We will look for someone who can help us figure this out. Given the holidays, I doubt we can find anyone this week, but we can call a psychologist next week and see what they think."

At that very moment, I was officially screwed.

Being next-level anxious, I began to obsess over the idea of being depressed. Focused very much on things I could not control, I started to read online about depression and got very little sleep in the process as my thoughts raced every night after that. Before you knew it, I was very much DEPRESSED. The words *self-fulfilling prophecy* couldn't accurately describe what had just gone down.

A few days after a very difficult New Year's Eve, during which I felt so anxious the entire time, I rang in the New Year crying in my mother's arms. Unfortunately, it was time to return to Ottawa to resume my final semester. I had officially made myself sick and had no idea how to finish a semester and the second part of a two-term internship at the Paul Menton Centre (PMC) for Students with Disabilities at Carleton University.

Yet, my family insisted. They told me I had to believe everything would be OK and that it would be. Probably some of the dumbest advice you can give a person suffering from depression, but my first episode hadn't really taught them the right or wrong thing to say when I am depressed, however mild, moderate, or severe the episode.

The anxiety persisted. The sleepless nights piled up, and the episode intensified. I cried every day and begged my family to let me return home, as there was no way I could get through that semester. I told my internship supervisor what was happening, and he suggested I take some time off to recover and regroup before deciding to drop the semester. I then spoke to the professors whose classes I was registered for, and they were also OK with my supervisor's suggestion to take a week or two to assess my situation. By nightfall, I was back in Montreal.

The more time I had to think, and the more time I was not being treated for my anxiety and sleep disturbance, the more things worsened and the more I leaned toward not going back. About a week later, Olga drove my car to Ottawa as I couldn't go very far without an emotional breakdown, and she didn't want me to risk my life or anyone else's. I dreaded going to my supervisor, as I felt like a complete failure and ashamed not to complete the second part of the internship they had hired me for. I was leaving them in a jam as all the students already had secured their internships by that point, and they wouldn't be able to find anyone else, contributing to my self-loathing quite a bit.

My supervisor, Boris, had a very hard time wrapping his head around what he heard me tell him as I already started accentuating my disabilities and speaking about being incapable of fulfilling what they needed for the semester. There was a sharp contrast between what he had seen me accomplish and what I reported about myself and my capabilities. He appeared saddened by what was happening and highlighted my great work the previous semester. For a moment, I felt bad, like perhaps I was making a big mistake—but that moment came and went because that's how the *monster* rolls.

That day continued to be very upsetting as I moved out of my apartment and said goodbye to my roommate, Maria, whom I considered a sister. I felt guilty for leaving her on such short notice that she couldn't rent out my room. I felt guilty for this happening to me again and for having to withdraw my studies from this university. I also felt guilty for leaving this one particular student behind at the Paul Menton Centre, a young man with schizophrenia who had connected with me in a way he hadn't with any other therapist.

I felt guilty for all the money my parents had spent on my education that the *monster* had already convinced me I was not even going to complete. I felt guilty for everything I had done throughout 2009 because, in my mind, it now appeared as if I truly didn't deserve any of it. I felt guilty for my existence, really ... and guilt is not only a symptom of depression but is majorly correlated with suicidal ideation.[2] The more guilt I felt, the more I hated myself; the more I hated myself, the more I started considering putting an end to my wretched life.

After being home for a week, the anxiety and guilt persisted, and the delusions inevitably began. I started realizing how dependent I had been on family for a lot of things until the age of twenty-six and fixated on this idea that if suddenly my parents and my brother all passed away, I wouldn't be able to survive, let alone make it in life. I started believing that because of my disabilities and my familial dependence, I would need to live in a center of some kind where I would be taken care of, which then led me to google the possibilities.

---

2. https://bpspsychub.onlinelibrary.wiley.com/doi/10.1111/bjc. 12291

In no time, I called the Douglas Mental Health Institute, and while extremely scared and crying hysterically, I asked if they could keep me—I pleaded with them, really.

My mom, who could hear me crying, came into my room, and out of fear, I hung up. What was I afraid of? Would she scold me again if I told her I had a problem? Maybe—because that painful experience from seven years prior had left a mark, and when feeling anxious, traumatic experiences rush to the fore, as do irrational fears.

I was practically choking from fear—fear of my mom not understanding that I needed to be placed, fear of her not wanting to take me to the Douglas, fear of her not getting me the kind of help the *monster* had convinced me I needed.

Quickly dropping to my knees as she approached my desk, I said, "Mom, please take me to the Douglas. Please, please, it's the only place that can take care of me."

"What are you saying? Take care of you? We are here for you; you don't have to go anywhere else!"

"Yes, but Ma, what if you die tomorrow?"

"Sophie!"

"What if you and Daddy and Tony all die in a car accident?"

"Sophie! Stop!"

"Mom, think about it, please. If you die, I can't live on my own. I can't do anything! Even if you leave me money or this house, I will not be able to manage it. I need someone to take care of me. PLEASE BELIEVE ME!"

"Sophie! I am not taking you to the Douglas. You're not crazy. Stop this nonsense. Wake up, please. Please wake up; this is not you. STOP!"

"Mom, I need help. Please."

"Yes, you do—that is clear to me now. We will get you help, but you are not going to the Douglas!"

She then helped me stand, hugged me, and asked me to leave my computer and my room, assuming that if "out of sight," this new idea would be "out of mind." My computer being out of sight, though, wouldn't make a difference because the *monster* had very much taken over my mind.

Later in the day, when my brother came home from work, I begged him to take me to the Douglas Hospital to lock me up permanently because of how convinced I was that I'd never be able to fend for myself, given I was "intellectually disabled" and all. My anxiety was through the roof that day, and I wasn't equipped with strategies to reduce it.

It wasn't clicking to me that the methods I taught my internship clients to manage their anger would also help me reduce my anxiety.

It's like whatever education and experience I had by that point had gone out the window, the anxiety too intense to think or see clearly.

And so, Tony agreed to take me to the Douglas, but while we waited in the emergency unit waiting room, he turned to me and said, "I'm not leaving you here. We're just waiting to see a doctor and make sure he gets it this time. There's NO WAY I'm leaving here without you today."

Though I was comforted knowing my brother was there for me, I still felt pretty anxious at the idea of not being kept there as the *monster* had me convinced *this* was the only way for me to get through life.

Dr. Farquhar eventually saw us. I told him my whole story and that he really needed to keep me there. While he validated my struggle, he couldn't disagree more with the option of admission to the psych ward. Telling me this didn't comfort me at all; it only reinforced the belief that no one understood me.

Yet, Dr. Farquhar understood me more than I knew because he could tell that the *monster* had me saying all this nonsense about being intellectually disabled, as it was absolutely impossible for an intellectually disabled person—however mild the disability—to have completed a bachelor's degree and 90 percent of her master's degree with straight A's. It was just not possible. With that incongruence alone, he knew I was majorly depressed, and delusions were, unfortunately, very much part of my current experience, an experience I would wish upon no one.

Dr. Farquhar prescribed medications that could help with my sleep, reduce my anxiety, and assist with my ADHD symptoms. The Ritalin I'd tried in 2003 resulted in unfortunate side effects. Hence, I never pursued taking it, and either way, it did nothing to aid with my auditory processing and memory challenges, so I didn't see the benefit in putting up with the side effects. This psychiatrist was not recommending something else and told me he would stick by me until we found the medication best suited for my ADHD. He also said it would be difficult to determine at present how effective this medication would be, given the depressive symptoms were as yet untreated. I was told to be patient and stay the course.

The *monster*, though, had other plans.

Before I knew it, I was signed up for an eight-week outpatient program at the Douglas. On my first day, I wondered how the hell I wound up there. There were individuals with severe mental illness who, in my mind, clearly could have benefited from this program. But me? I wasn't mentally ill, I was "retarded."[3] What could this program possibly offer *me*?

I remember feeling very uncomfortable and unable to warm up to anyone, which is odd since I usually jump into groups and start

---

3. See prologue

chatting away. I wanted nothing to do with anyone in the program. It is set up in a manner that provides a lot of valuable group therapy, something I'd observed during internships when I had co-facilitated various therapy groups.

Can you imagine knowing you did all that, but your mind consistently works against you and convinces you otherwise? I would like you to pause from reading this book for one minute and actively try to convince yourself that you are incapable of doing one thing you know you're good at. As odd as this sounds, pretend you're in front of a judge, and you need to convince him that you are incapable of doing the one thing that pretty much everyone knows you are capable of doing as if you were trying to do everything in your power to prove your innocence. Take a moment and do this.

A little off-putting, isn't it?

Imagine doing this practically every waking minute of your day for a solid six months. As I write, I think back to how much I experienced this and what a nightmare it was to live like this, especially in the last major depressive episode that went on for thirteen brutal months.

Back to the Douglas, about four days into the program, I already couldn't take it anymore. I went home and wrote my first-ever suicide letter. While attending the program those first few days, I hated it so much that I envisioned driving my red G35 into the St. Lawrence River. While I was at the center, whenever we could view our phones, I searched how difficult it is to free oneself from a submerged vehicle and how long it takes before one completely drowns. I was convinced this was my best way out, and so when I wrote the suicide note, the intention was to drive into the river the next morning as I didn't want to attend that center another minute.

Knowing my intention for the next day, I didn't sleep well that night. I was scared of what I had set out to do and woke up a couple of times an hour as my body progressively felt like it was on fire. It's important to note that the medication I'd started, well, some of it might have helped me sleep, but the rest would not really kick in until two to three weeks later.

When I woke up, I burst out crying and called my brother to come home from work. Thank God he worked for the family business. Thank God he had the leeway to drop everything whenever I needed him. I would have otherwise cost him his job if he were employed by anyone else, and that would've added even more guilt to an already overflowing plate.

My brother found me hiding under my bedcovers, bundled in a fetal position. He lifted my covers and asked me what was going on. I pointed at my desk, and he picked up the suicide note. Make no mistake, my asking him to read my letter was not a cry for attention—it was a cry for "I really don't wanna die, so please make sure I don't die today."

I peeked out from under the blankets and saw tears rolling down my brother's face. He felt anxious, which physically manifested itself in his gagging. After reading the letter, he cried and asked, "Why would you do this to us? Why? How could you? Don't you realize Mom and Dad will die if you do this?"

"I'm sorry, T."

"Sorry? Sorry? This isn't one of those times *sorry* is going to cut it, kid."

"I'm really scared, T. I don't wanna die."

"And there's no f*ckin' way I'll let that happen. Get dressed now. I'm taking you back to the emergency."

Chapter Four

Humanity: 1. The Monster: 0

As IF MY BROTHER's day hadn't already been difficult enough, he sat there with me in the emergency department of the Douglas Hospital for about six hours before we were finally seen by Dr. Farquhar. He continued to be patient with me and my persistence regarding being mentally challenged.

Dr. Farquhar did his best to reassure me that in due time when I recovered from this depressive episode, I would notice a very big difference in my attention, concentration, and memory as a result of the depressive symptoms subsiding and the prescribed ADHD medication going into full effect.

I, though, continued to believe that I had more than ADHD and learning disabilities. I was so exasperated that I couldn't get anyone else to believe this that I just nodded my agreement so we could get the hell out of there. But since I had been brought in after presenting my brother with a suicide note, it was grounds for me to be admitted for at least twenty-four hours for my own safety.

I tried to remain as composed as possible when the doctor brought this up. He also said the only way I could go home was if my brother signed, and he would take full responsibility for my safety that night.

My brother looked at me, then the doctor, and asked if we could take a moment or two to think. We stepped out of Dr. Farquhar's office and went back into that dreadful waiting room, and I said, "F*ck! Are you kidding me? I can't go home?"

"Sophs ... calm down," my brother said.

"No, I can't calm down. I don't want to sleep here tonight, damn it!"

"Well, I guess you should have thought of that before writing a suicide note and putting us through f*ckin' hell today. Mom has struggled at the store without me while freaking out about what you considered doing and what is going to happen next. And I have wasted another f*ckin' day, so when I tell you to calm down, calm the f*ck down so we can figure this out."

Shaken by what he said, I looked down at the floor as I could no longer look him in the eye. "I'm sorry."

"Already told you sorry wasn't going to cut it. Do I have your word that you're not going to try offing yourself tonight?"

I thought to myself that if I were to do this, it would certainly not be tonight and certainly not on his watch.

"I promise, T. I'm too tired to do anything at this point. I promise I won't do anything. I'll even sleep in your room if it makes you feel better. Just don't leave me here."

"You have no idea what kind of position you're putting me in. If you do something on my watch, I will never recover from that, you hear me?"

Feeling so bad at the idea of him blaming himself for my suicide, I continued to swear that I would not do anything that night. It was almost as if I was engaged in an internal negotiation with the *monster* for me never to do anything on my brother's watch.

"I hear you, T. Loud and clear. Again, I'm sorry."

After my brother signed the forms handed to him by Dr. Farquhar, we were finally allowed to leave. On the ride home, I asked Tony if it was possible for me to go straight to my room or his and not have to talk to Mom and Dad about what had happened that day. Guilt and shame had started seeping in, but I also couldn't handle being misunderstood any further. I knew there was no way I could get through to my mom about my actions—there was no way I could do anything for her to understand. I honestly had nothing left in me at that point to even bother trying.

Luckily, Tony didn't feel compelled to punish me for my actions and agreed that we should skip out on an encounter with my mom and that he would have a conversation with her to calm her down while I was in his room.

Despite everything I had put him through, my big brother was still very willing to protect his little sister and minimize her suffering.

The next day, Tony did not leave for work in the morning. He drove me directly to the outpatient center himself. I was not looking forward to my encounter with the psychologist and the staff, as clearly they had been informed of my actions of the prior day. But, truth be told, they welcomed me with open arms and didn't make the situation awkward at all. Clearly, I wasn't the only patient in their eight-week program to have ever tried something like this.

Also, something that was clear to me is that a lot of the other patients in the program were seasoned, and there was no fooling *them* or avoiding their questioning regarding my not having shown up the day before. I was truly a mystery to a lot of them. On the one hand, they believed what I told them about being intellectually challenged and that perhaps I didn't belong there. On the other hand, I would confuse the hell out of them when I found myself occasionally finishing the sentences of the group facilitators, which is exactly what happened that day.

While in one of the groups just before lunch, as the facilitator demonstrated a tool often used in cognitive behavioral therapy (CBT), one of the patients expressed having a hard time understanding how to apply what they had just been taught. I noticed that after the facilitator gave it another go, the patient still hadn't really fully understood. I instinctively stepped in and started to demonstrate a certain principle in a different way, using an example that would really drive things home. Needless to say, I had the entire group of patients, including the facilitator and her assistant, stumped—and the funny thing is, it wasn't at all obvious to me why that was the case.

Here I was, practically begging them on a daily basis to believe that I was intellectually disabled rather than depressed and that I did not belong there—and the only truth they could now see was that I didn't belong there as a patient but as a group therapist.

The facilitator then asked me to explain a certain aspect of CBT even further, and I didn't hesitate to do so because I thoroughly enjoyed this approach for the first three-quarters of my master's education. As I did this, the psychologist got all the proof they needed that I was very much depressed and that this idea of being intellectually disabled was a delusion more than anything—a delusion the *monster* had fabricated and thoroughly ingrained in my mind.

They pointed out to me what I had just done, hoping I would realize that I am actually not that challenged and that in due time, I will be OK and on my way back to completing my master's and helping people improve their mental health ... save their lives, even.

For the first time since this all began, I felt hopeful, and for a very short moment, I believed what they said—a very short moment, though, because within seconds, the *monster* had stripped me of that hope and had me convinced I was a fraud.

The truth is, I had not stopped fantasizing about driving my car into the river. A couple of days later, I woke up determined just finally to do it. I felt some relief with this decision, and even though

I would likely be met with psychological resistance when I headed to my destination, I was still oddly relieved with my decision—or so I thought.

Throughout the day, my subconscious dropped little hints, making comments like, "This won't matter too much, anyway," or "It will all be over soon." Little did I know that one of the other group members was paying very close attention to the crap coming out of my mouth that day.

Just before the day was over, in the last group counseling session, the facilitator asked if there was anything I wanted to share with the group. I was a little taken aback by this sudden hot-seat situation and quickly said, "No." Then, I was asked if I'd had any thoughts of suicide that day. That's when I was really stumped. For a second, I wondered if there was a chip in my head recording my plan. My hesitance to respond seemed to confirm what the facilitator suspected. Meanwhile, she wasn't the only one who picked up on what was happening. One of my group mates did, too, and, out of concern, quickly signaled this to the facilitator.

When the facilitator told me that the other patient expressed this concern and wanted to make sure I didn't hurt myself after I left the program, I could not hold back my tears. What I thought was relief earlier in the day paled compared to the relief I experienced at that moment—at least, that's what my body demonstrated with this release of tears.

Like I have said before, when depressed, deep down, we really don't want to die—we want the pain to end. We want the mental torment to *stop*. The *monster* persuades us that death is the only way that will happen, but it's not! The patient who reported his concerns to the facilitator had already been in the program for seven weeks and had seen for himself that things do get better. He, too, was on the brink of suicide in the past, and he regularly considered it at the beginning of the program as well. He told me that he saw himself in me, and his gut told him that I was in danger.

I'd never had a person who barely knew me display such humanity. I broke down and shared with the entire group what I planned to do once the day at the center was over. Some were in shock, others had most certainly heard worse, and the patient in question was relieved, knowing he did the right thing by expressing his concerns. I was scared out of my wits. I had read enough about what drowning feels like that my chosen method to end my life was definitely anxiety-provoking.

The group then made me promise I wouldn't drive my car into the river. Unlike the occasion when I promised my brother I wouldn't attempt to die on his watch, I knew I would do so off his watch; this time, no such thought entered my mind. Humanity: 1. The *monster*: 0.

It's very important to note that from the start of the program until the very end, my best friend Olga (who later became family as a result of my being the religious witness at her wedding and eventually the godmother of her first child) came over after work every single day and just sat on the couch in the basement with me for hours. Five days a week, for at least three months. What could we have to say to each other on a daily basis, especially given I was that depressed and repeating the same spiel over and over?

NOTHING.

She sat with me in silence—and that was OK. More than OK, it contributed to my staying alive during that episode. She was there, on the couch with me, watching whatever show popped up. Imagine that: skimming through channels for a few hours and hoping to land on the occasional movie. But none of that mattered to her or me. What mattered was that she didn't force me to speak, she didn't judge me when I actually did speak, and she didn't try to fix me. She was just present.

People underestimate the value of being *present* for a friend or loved one in times of distress, especially during depressive episodes. I have had people disappear on me during these episodes simply because they didn't know what to say—so they chose to say and do nothing. As a result of these brutal experiences, I've recognized who really matters in my life.

But is it fair to say that, though, when I know that most of the planet is sorely uneducated about this topic, and the conversation is far from normalized? Years later, I realized it wasn't fair to say that … and if I harbored resentment toward anyone who disappeared during those difficult times of my life, that's because *my shoulds* contributed to this. All I could do was share my story and teach people what they could do if this ever happened again or if it happened to anyone else they cared about.

This is a good time for me to share ways you can help someone you care about who is suffering from depression and also what to avoid doing or saying when choosing to offer help. Furthermore, I would like to equip you with the tools to intervene if ever someone presents you with thoughts of suicide or if you suspect they are considering harming themselves.

I am not in any way proposing you cross your boundaries and limits and indirectly become a therapist here. However, saying the right thing at the right time—before your loved one then hopefully gets professional help—might save their life.

Recently, when talking to one of my best friends, she questioned whether she did the right thing during the last depressive episode. I realized during our conversation that sharing valuable strategies gained during fifty hours of training from Suicide Action Montreal (S.A.M.) might help readers intervene over the phone with suicidal individuals. When people call the crisis line because they're concerned about someone they know possibly attempting suicide, we do not train the callers to act as therapists.

As such, I repeat: My goal here is not to train you to become one, nor is it to apply any pressure on you to take on such a role. Rather, it is best to defer to a mental health professional.

With that disclaimer out of the way, the following are tips to help you be a source of support for a friend or relative with depression, including what to avoid in the process.

- **Start a conversation—whether it's in person, over the phone, or even via text message.** I'm all about authenticity and real talk, and I think that's the best way to go, so rather than beat around the bush and delay the inevitable, get straight to the point and express your concern. The sooner you do, the sooner you show the person in question you care and that you're there for them. The sooner you deepen your connection, the sooner you get one to open up. Focus on using "I" statements when expressing your feelings to them. Essentially, take ownership of your feelings, and don't point fingers at them by making statements such as, "You haven't been yourself lately," "You seem to be avoiding hanging out with us lately," or "You are worrying me lately." "You" statements typically create defensiveness all around, and not just in those who are depressed. Consider beginning a sentence with "I'm worried," "I'm concerned," or "I have been wondering" instead of with a "you" statement. Chances are, the person will feel cared about and will, in turn, open up to you.

Keep in mind that the person may want to talk about what they feel, but they might not want advice. Typically, we just want to be heard. Even in my case, where my situation was extreme, and I insisted no one could ever help me, given my intellectual disability, I still felt good when I heard. Can't speak so much for the other person doing the hearing, but if you follow my advice and let go of trying to fix your friend or relative, you will feel significantly less helpless when listening to them.

Engage with your friend by asking questions to get more information instead of assuming you understand what they mean. Show interest using your body language as well. Validating their feelings is helpful in fostering a better connection; don't tell them they don't know what they're talking about or that what they're saying is absurd, because believe me, I heard that all too often, which led me to no longer respond to messages or calls from said friend. Subsequently, this resulted in further isolation and time spent in my head.

Also, I would suggest you have an in-person conversation whenever possible and/or at least a video chat. Although your friend may not like talking the first time you ask, it can help to continue telling them you care. If they end up talking about their depression, please don't minimize or compare their experience to someone else's struggle. Telling them things could be so much worse or demonstrating what you perceive as worse situations generally doesn't help. I can vouch that this was absolutely the biggest turnoff for me and led me to shut the person out completely.

Pro tip: Even someone who is not depressed but is merely going through a hard time does NOT want to be told things could be worse, so don't do it. To learn more about unhelpful listening behaviors in general, check out my mini-course on communication, available at www.alive316.com.

- **Continue learning about depression on your own.** Reading this book is definitely a great start, and if you ever know of someone else who has a friend or family member struggling with depression, lend them this book, or better yet, get them to buy it so they can also put it on their coffee table and contribute to normalizing the conversation. There's more to learn beyond this book as people experience depression differently, but familiarity with the general symptoms and terminology definitely facilitates a more in-depth conversation with your friend.

Learning about depression also means your friend or loved one won't have to explain what they're experiencing over and over, which is exhausting. No need to become an expert here, but do not go into that conversation completely oblivious either because you will likely do more harm than good. Yes, depression often involves sadness or low mood, but it often also involves anger and irritability, excessive fatigue or sleep concerns (exacerbated by feeling anger a lot), difficulties with memory and/or concentration (zoning out is pretty normal here), and physical symptoms, such as headaches, stomach distress, and muscle pain, often brought on by excessive anxiety present during a depressive episode. You can have anxiety without depression, but rarely can an individual have depression without anxiety.

To make things easier, I will propose an acronym that I learned during my postgraduate studies that has served as a useful mnemonic to remember the symptoms of depression. Many in my field have found this helpful, as have others I've introduced it to:

SIGECAPS! Pronounced "SIG-E-CAPS." Here is what each letter in SIGECAPS stands for:

- **S**leep disturbance: Finds it difficult to fall asleep and stay asleep during the night. Can also have excessive daytime sleepiness or even sleep too much.

- **I**nterest: Decreased or lost interest in previously enjoyed activities, as well as a decreased ability to feel pleasure.

- **G**uilt feelings: Excessive guilt, even for no reason, and feelings of worthlessness can cause sufferers to believe they're a burden to loved ones and those around them.

- **E**nergy loss: No longer having the energy to do things and feeling fatigued with little to no motivation. Symptoms, such as sadness and emptiness, further exacerbate feelings of fatigue.

- **C**oncentration problems: Attention and memory, as well

as information processing and decision-making skills, are impaired.

- **A**ppetite changes: Some individuals with depression manifest increased appetite, while others lose their appetite.

- **P**sychomotor functioning (decreased): There is a slowing down or hampering of one's mental or physical activities. This is typically seen as slow thinking or slow body movements.

- **S**uicidal ideation: Often called suicidal thoughts or ideas, this is a broad term used to describe a range of contemplations, wishes, and preoccupations with death and suicide. Thoughts about harming oneself or taking one's own life are essentially present.

The purpose of SIGECAPS is to help people identify the symptoms of depression in themselves or others. It is important to remember that not everyone experiences all the symptoms on this list. Some people may only experience a few, while others may experience many.

- **Get therapist referrals.** As you learn more about depression, you will discover more support and treatments for it. We've reached a point where more people than not believe therapy can help, but it is sometimes intimidating to search for a therapist and make an appointment. If you know of a therapist who can provide referral options, that is always helpful. It is worth mentioning that establishing a connection with one's therapist can take a couple of sessions.

If ever your friend tells you they don't like or feel comfortable with their therapist, changing therapists is the more suitable option than dropping the idea of therapy altogether. If you don't know a mental health professional personally, you can always offer to help your friend review potential professionals and encourage them to make that first appointment. If they are already in therapy, encourage them to stick with it whenever they feel like canceling. After a week or so of overthinking and draining the brain, we forget how productive or useful our previous session was. Encourage your friend to stay the course, as this truly is a case where "slow and steady wins the race."

- **Focus on what you can control.** This helps you feel more empowered, and doing the opposite breeds helplessness. One thing you can control during someone else's depressive episode is offering to help with everyday tasks. As I mentioned above, energy and psychomotor function are impacted when depressed. As a result, many have a hard time doing day-to-day tasks, such as grocery shopping, laundry, or paying bills. Simple activities that otherwise don't require too much thought suddenly become overwhelming. Flat out, ask your friend, "What do you need the most help with today?" If you notice that your friend or relative is behind on household chores, find a way to tackle a specific task together, as having your company can make the work seem less challenging.

Another thing in your control is letting your friend or relative know you still care about them even when you're unable to spend time with them on a regular basis. Sending a quick text saying you've been thinking about and caring for them as they continue to work through depression can be really helpful. On many occasions, especially in a more recent depressive episode, such texts even saved my life. There were moments when I was about to attempt suicide or heavily considering it, and a text came in from a friend checking on me and changed everything.

Depressed people might withdraw more to avoid reaching out, so don't feel surprised or take it personally if you're suddenly doing more work to maintain your friendship. Even if they won't express it to you at the moment, continuing to be a positive and supportive presence may make all the difference to them, possibly even save their life as it did for me. If that's not a good enough reason for you to stick around, I'm not sure what is.

Another thing individuals with depression find difficult is keeping plans. I recall canceling plans quite often, which would only add to my feelings of guilt, thereby making me hate my life even more. When someone cancels plans as often as I did, it can lead to people giving up, as was also the case with me and some folks. People typically stop inviting the depressed person to places, and they stop trying to include them, which worsens feelings of depression.

Going back to what you can control in all this, don't take it personally when an invitation gets canceled or a phone call goes ignored.

Another thing you can control is accepting in advance that they're unlikely to accept an invite. Some of my good friends had gotten used to it and, luckily, never gave up trying because there actually was a slight chance I would say yes, depending on who else would be present and what environment we would be going to. Once you've accepted the above and understand there's nothing personal about all this, continue to extend invitations and let your friend know you understand that they may not be able to keep plans during this difficult time. Let them know there's no pressure to come out, and you'll be happy to see them whenever they feel more up to socializing. That last part makes a world of difference to a person who has become obsessed with dying, like I had.

Every time I think I'll pause on giving you tips to better handle a situation involving depression, I find myself wanting to share more insight. Of course, I cannot cover everything here, and reaching out to me for a consultation on how to best deal with your situation is an option, but until then, I want to add this one last thing. Nonjudgmentally, imagine yourself in your friend's position. Consider how you would feel and how you would want friends to respond if you were dealing with depressive symptoms, and trust me when I say that self-disclosure can be extremely effective if you have personally experienced depression. By being vulnerable and admitting your understanding, you will give your friend or family member the gift of relief.

I have seen this firsthand while self-disclosing in my sessions over the years before I made my story available to the public through social media. I have seen it with the feedback I receive through private messages after live sharing parts of my story, and I certainly saw it when I shared it with a friend who was considering suicide and was experiencing depression at the level that I had.

Just be there *with* the person rather than *for* the person. Even if they push you away, let them know you're in it *with* them.

On a side note, please remember that it's OK to take space for yourself if you feel emotionally drained. You may need to consider talking with a therapist or other supportive individual in your life about how you feel, but I cannot stress enough how much patience is required. Depression usually improves with treatment, but it can take time and entail some trial and error. Even a successful course of treatment does not guarantee a complete recovery from depression, and your loved one may occasionally still experience symptoms. They'll undoubtedly experience both good and bad days in this unpleasant process, so don't assume a good day implies they're "fixed." Please try not to lose patience if it seems like they will never get better after a few consecutive bad days. I know I threw a few people off because of some of the good days I had.

There is no clear time frame for healing from depression, and it won't help either of you if you anticipate that they will feel like themselves again after a few weeks of therapy. Make the best of the good days and actively practice gratitude for the good in each other's lives. I suggest you both practice gratitude as it can be very helpful, given the effect of doing so on reducing stress hormones.[1]

You will unquestionably experience more stress when someone you love is experiencing depression, so it's also important to take care of your own needs. If you put all your energy into supporting the person you care about, you'll have very little left for yourself and won't be much help to anyone if you are burning out or feeling angry.

Knowing your limits and setting boundaries is never more important than during a time when the *monster* has presented itself in your inner circle. Setting limits with the person is not only beneficial but crucial. Let the person know, for instance, that you're available to talk once you get home from work, but not before, and if you're worried they'll think they can't get in touch with you, offer to assist them in developing a backup plan in case they do need you during your working hours. This may entail locating a hotline they can dial or creating a code word they can text you in an emergency.

Instead of attempting to assist daily, you might offer to drop by every other day or perhaps deliver dinner twice a week. Consider including

---

1. https://health.ucdavis.edu/medicalcenter/features/2015-2016 /11/20151125_gratitude.html

other friends to create a bigger support network for both of you, really, because, as one of my best friends recently told me, it was very helpful for her to have a game plan with another good friend of mine. She reported that when they came together to see me, it was more helpful as they were able to debrief with each other afterward. If they could not make it together, the other person would be there for the absent person via call post-visit. Again, remember, the depression I experienced was pretty major and intense, so having such game plans in place might not be necessary for you if someone you love is dealing with a milder form, but still, it's a great option in case you need it. Please make sure to take care of yourself in this process. I'm equally a proponent of preventing caregivers from burning out and becoming depressed as I am of normalizing the conversation surrounding depression.

When things get scary, as in there are possible thoughts or even talk of suicide, indications that your person may be seriously contemplating suicide include:

- talking about death or dying

- buying a weapon

- engaging in more risky or harmful activities

- giving away belongings or donating priceless items

- pushing people away while saying goodbye with more emotion than usual

- talking about feeling trapped and/or wanting a way out

If you believe your friend or loved one is considering suicide, encourage them to call their therapist while you are with them or ask them if you can make the call on their behalf. If the therapist doesn't answer, encourage your friend to send a text that the therapist can see between sessions. I highly recommend you stay with them if the therapist hasn't answered the call, and encourage them to text or call a crisis line. With a simple Google search, you will be able to find the best-suited organization to call in your area.

Depending on the severity of your friend's thoughts, you might need to take them straight to the hospital emergency room or, at the very least, stay with them as long as you can until they stop feeling suicidal. Again, I don't expect you to become an expert just from reading this book, and I honestly don't ask that you become one either unless the mental health field is the direction you're aiming to go in life.

If you're worried about bringing up the subject of suicide as it might be triggering for them, don't be. Trust your intuition. If something feels off about their recent behavior and you've noticed any of the bullet points mentioned above, discussing it is generally beneficial and often a lifesaver.

In order to determine the severity of the situation, find out if they have given it serious thought. I will outline below how you can do so from the training I received in 2008 when I volunteered at Suicide Action Montreal (S.A.M.). This training was for people not in the mental health field, and I truly wish it would be offered as often as CPR is offered to people who are not in the medical field.

Direct questions about suicide include:

1. "Are you having suicidal thoughts?"

2. "Have you felt like you want to end your life?"

These questions can help someone talk about how they are feeling. If the person answers yes to either of these questions, here is what I suggest you say next:

1. "Have you thought about how you might do this?"

2. "Have you had any intention of acting on these thoughts of killing yourself, as opposed to you having the thoughts, but you definitely would not act on them?"

3. "Have you started to work out, or have you worked out the details of how to kill yourself? Do you intend to carry out this plan?"

4. "In the past three months, have you done anything, started to do anything, or prepared to do anything to end your life?" (You never know when their actual depressive episode began, so although it may seem like it's fairly recent, looks can often deceive in this case. I would ask this regardless of when you think their troubles started.)

The answers to these questions will very much paint a greater picture of the intensity of the situation.

If they tell you it crossed their mind once, on the one hand, I want to say there's no need to rush them over to the emergency or to call 911. On the other hand, however, if their depression is major (you'll know by how much they belittle themselves and try to convince you of things that are simply not true), then I would take them to the emergency department.

Things grow more worrisome when a person has a plan of some kind that involves a method, location, and date. If there's a method and location, the really important question next is if they already have what they need for the method in mind and if they have a date. If they plan on doing so within the next twenty-four hours, then they've likely put serious thought into this for some time, something I can most certainly vouch for once again, and immediate action needs to be taken.

If they refuse to let you take them to the emergency room, call the suicide helpline in your area and let them know what's going on. If the lines are clogged, call 911. Before calling 911, though, if you have it in you to be a little deceiving and are willing to tell them you will take them somewhere else, like for a drive to clear your mind and/or a drive-through for comfort food, and then you take them to the emergency instead (or right after), then do that! I personally think there's nothing wrong with a little deception if it increases your chances of saving someone's life. Will this affect how much they trust you during the rest of the episode? Quite possibly. If you know there are others who can show support and be there for the person after they've left the ER, then I would do it.

If you're truly the only person in their circle being supportive, then I would call the helpline and have them do the rest. Either way, after your friend recovers from depression and this monster no longer clouds their judgment, they will let go of their anger toward you for "deceiving" them and thank you for going that far to save their life.

In the case where your loved one doesn't have a plan or date, the severity of the situation is often lesser, and this is where you can essentially take some time and accentuate their reasons to live.

Take a look at Figure 1 below—the black square with a little white triangle in the corner. The white triangle symbolizes how much your loved one with suicidal thoughts believes they have a reason to live. The rest of the black square symbolizes how much more they are pulled toward ending their life. When you're talking with your person, help them focus on *their* reasons for living and avoid trying to impose *your* reasons for them to stay alive; this is most certainly not the time to guilt the person, so please be sure to keep your "shoulds" in check!

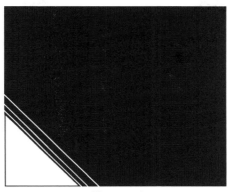

Figure 1

Listen carefully for what they say is their reason to live, or listen for them to express guilt about someone they recognize would be negatively impacted if they went through with ending their life. Work from this, and maybe along the way, another reason to live will be unearthed. Be a bit of a detective—ask questions pertaining to the people they mention, and don't hesitate to take them in the direction of sharing great memories they've had with said person and the possibility of creating more memorable moments in the future.

Your mission before getting off the phone or leaving your loved one's home is to move that line in the triangle just a bit higher, essentially making it so the triangle represents that their desire to live has increased even slightly.

This can very much contribute to them holding on longer because they would be reminded that they do, in fact, matter. Asking your loved one to promise they won't put any of their thoughts into action also can help save their life. Provided the depression isn't as severe as the episodes I have described thus far, that promise can go a long way.

If you happen to be reading this book while experiencing depression and suicidal thinking, you're truly not as alone as you feel. I understand how suicide might seem like the only method of relief—believe me, I do. Your life most certainly matters to at least one person, though, and I truly hope my story helps you hang on until you have fully recovered.

When you do recover, I look forward to hearing from you and will welcome you to join me in this Movement of **H**elping **O**pen **P**eople's **E**yes. We can do so much together, provided you give your life another chance. Promise me you will allow us to meet and discuss how we have both beaten this *monster*.

Promise?

Chapter Five

"If You Do This Again, You WILL Kill Him"

AT THE BEGINNING OF this book, I told you about the suicide attempt I survived on March 16, 2011. Now, let me tell you what led to this heart-wrenching day.

Freshly into 2011, about six weeks after completing my master's degree, I was interviewed for an entry-level counseling position for Lifeworks (then part of Ceridian Canada). This resource program helps employees manage personal issues at work or home. I had decided early on in 2011 that I would stay in Ottawa for at least another year until I got whatever paperwork and extra courses completed to be able to practice in the province of Quebec. Also, not going to lie; I actually liked my life in Ottawa, as strange as that may sound to most Montrealers.

The interview went well. Those couple of years of volunteer experience in multiple organizations across Montreal, including S.A.M., appeared to have paid off. The interviewers were impressed with the kind of crisis situations I found myself handling, even before I had completed my training as a counselor at a graduate level.

By the end of the interview, they asked me if I foresaw any challenges with this job. Given everything I had already described as being able to handle, nothing came to mind.

They asked if I was prepared to wait a month until the next paid training, and I gave a definite yes. Before I knew it, I had a job with a great company and a decent starting salary that I never would've seen in the province of Quebec, with benefits, not too far from home, in a field I was passionate about. Life was good!

Or so I thought ...

As I celebrated with my roommate Maria, I began describing to her what the job entailed, and it dawned on me hard and fast that I had not mentioned in the interview that I have ADHD and learning disabilities, including an auditory processing disorder.

Why would that last part specifically matter so much? Well, I would be required to perform my duties as an intake and crisis counselor in a cubicle in a room with many others taking calls at the same time—yet I could barely, if at all, block out the background noise of any kind when spoken to.

When you spoke to me, if someone else was talking in the room, or there was music playing or some kind of noise, however soft or loud, I could not process the information entering my brain. I got through my bachelor's degree at McGill University with very specific and significant accommodations from the Office for Students with Disabilities, including having someone else take notes for me throughout all my classes and taking my exams in a room with no one else but an invigilator. Taking an exam in an auditorium with a few hundred others was impossible for me. The mere tap of someone's pencil on their desk would sabotage my performance.

When studying at the library for endless hours, I had to move around to different areas because just as I'd adjust to a quiet spot, someone else would sit close, ruining my ability to process the information I read in a chapter the minute they typed on their laptop or produced any kind of noise.

How on earth would I work in a sea of cubicles with another twenty to thirty people? How would I listen to callers express their distress for eight hours a day, with so many coworkers around me talking simultaneously when I couldn't get through a couple of minutes of talking with someone when a lot was happening around me? I had mastered the art of pretending to understand and say a word or two of confirmation/validation over the years not to appear stupid, a coping mechanism a lot of people with learning disabilities develop. But this was not going to be an option while on the job—a very serious job that involved a lot of listening.

A wave of anxiety overcame me. Panic set in, and the negative self-talk began. "Wait a minute ... Maria! I didn't tell them about having ADHD and learning disabilities. Damnit! They asked me if I foresaw any challenges with this job, and I said, 'No, not really. I have helped people with suicidal thoughts and plans before over the phone, which has very much prepared me for this type of work.' F*ck!"

Maria said, "What's the problem then, Sophs? You've been able to work over the phone before. Why are you panicking?"

"Because at the suicide helpline, there were only two other people maximum working, and we didn't always have calls at the same time. I only had one four-hour shift per week. On the off-chance that two calls came in, I would block one ear with my fingers as much as possible, but that was a draining experience every time, and I can't pull that off for an eight-hour shift with back-to-back calls all week long."

"Sophie, everything's going to be OK. The first month is training, anyway. Just see how it goes, and try to see how they might accommodate you."

"They can't accommodate me, Maria. This isn't university. This is the real f*ckin' world. No one has patience for people with learning disabilities and ADHD. I wrote a ten-page paper last semester on the topic and read a lot about all the challenges that arise in the workplace. I'm f*cked. I won't be able to do this."

"Please, you need to breathe."

Breathing didn't seem to be an option at that point. I felt like a fraud, and the idea that I misled them in the interview troubled me so much that my cortisol levels were through the roof. All I wanted to do was throw up rather than celebrate getting a new job.

Over the next few days, I was very preoccupied with variables I could not control. Doom and gloom appeared to be lurking on the horizon when they, in fact, were not. Unfortunately, one can create a depressive episode just by focusing on what they can't control.

Needless to say, this is what happened. I soon began to lose sleep, to have recurring, unhelpful negative thoughts, and to break down crying every time I thought about eventually starting this job as such an impostor.

This feeling of *impostor syndrome* can be very difficult to move past. It's an awful feeling and can be extremely isolating. It didn't matter that family and friends were showing support and willing to listen; I felt incredibly alone and incapable of doing this job and living my adult life independently. Before I knew it, those same damn obsessive thoughts from the year before, during the second depressive episode, were back.

Then it occurred to me that whatever I had been so worried about the year before during the depressive episode had not actually been resolved. I was still "mentally challenged." I was still "retarded."[1] I completely overlooked that I had gone back to the University of Ottawa to complete the final semester of my master's, and for that to happen (and to even make it into a master's program), it was impossible for me to be intellectually disabled. Well, it's not

---

1. See prologue

that I forgot—it's that the *monster* thoroughly convinced me of the impossible, that I was truly a fraud throughout all my studies.

It was back with a vengeance, and I found myself operating as if I was at least mildly intellectually challenged.

I convinced myself that I couldn't even shop for new clothing for my upcoming job, that I needed my mom to go shopping, and that I couldn't do this without her. Maria offered to shop with me so I could get a new wardrobe—for the job I already believed I would not be alive for. The thoughts of suicide had returned, louder than ever.

My brother and my mom started to suspect that I was going down that path again but desperately hoped that after I finished the first day of training, perhaps I would find a solution for accommodation and my anxiety would decrease or subside altogether. Talk about wishful thinking. The anxiety was so bad, and the obsessiveness about being intellectually disabled was so intense that there was no way I could explore options for accommodation. Instead, I explored possible options for death. I read, and I read, and I planned, and I planned.

Day one of Lifeworks' training was officially upon me. That morning, I felt intense heat throughout my body. I don't even know how I was capable of driving myself there, but I did, and when I walked into the building, one of the people who had interviewed me could tell right off the bat that something was not right. The look on my face and the energy I had in the interview versus what it was now was night and day. And yet, I lied through my teeth and insisted I was excited to start!

My body was on fire for the entire eight hours I was there, which was overwhelming and scary. I couldn't focus, absolutely no information registering throughout the day, and all I wrote on my notepad during the training was a suicide note. There was no way I was going to endure another day like this. No way.

So, at the end of my shift, I set out to park my car in a remote area not too far from home and mustered the courage to ingest an entire bottle of Tylenol.

I didn't expect messages and calls from my brother and mother, who had driven in from Montreal to pick me up from Ottawa. That mother's intuition I spoke about in Chapter 1? Yeah, she had a pretty bad feeling things were a lot worse than the year before, so she and Tony waited for me at my roommate's home to pack up my stuff so I could move back home with them right then and there.

My plans to live in Ottawa for the first few years of my career were officially undone, and that disappointment in itself fueled the *monster* who continued to tell me I should die.

Things only worsened over the next couple of weeks in Montreal as I felt tremendous guilt for the fact that I had left Ottawa again on unpleasant terms. I never saw it as "I left because I needed to recover" but instead as "I left because I'm an intellectually disabled fraud who will never make it in life." Fixate and obsess on that kind of belief for two weeks straight; recovery is the last thing that will happen.

In fact, another way one can exacerbate current depressive symptoms or even *create* a depressive episode is by focusing on variables they cannot control. I talk about this all the time in my courses and workshops. Focus long enough on variables you can't control, and you will feel very helpless. The more you obsess, the more anxious and frustrated you feel, the more depleted you'll become. The more fatigued you become, your anxiety and anger will, in turn, intensify—and then guess what? A vicious cycle has officially begun, and you're well on your way to developing depression.

Things out of our control include the past and future, yet people find themselves caught up in both. Focus instead on what you CAN control, and watch how empowered you will feel!

Going back to the last depressive episode, the obsession and hyper-focus led to an insufferable level of helplessness and hopelessness. To top it all off, an event was coming up that, before this episode, I'd very much looked forward to. One of my favorite musicians from the island of Crete was coming to play for our association's annual dance. March 12, 2011, was a date I had plugged into my calendar three months prior and had vowed not to miss. I had booked a ten-seater table for my parents, friends from Montreal, and friends who would drive in from out of town.

The days before the event, I made it clear that I didn't want to go. However, my mother would not have it. As if guilt wasn't already eating me alive, she added even more and reinforced that I "should" come. She wasn't aiming to make my suffering worse—if anything, she hoped it would lift my spirits to attend this event. And it did, actually, for a total of seven minutes.

I know seven minutes sounds very specific, but that's about the average time my favorite Cretan dance lasts. I barely said a word the entire night, unintentionally making most of the people at our table uncomfortable. Meanwhile, anxiety was tearing up my insides, and all I wanted to do was scream. Let's just say I was the "elephant at the table."

But at one point, when my favorite seven-minute Cretan dance, a *maleviziotis,* came on again, I couldn't resist. I ran to the dance floor and joined my friends in the circle. Most were shocked, and a minute or so later, a friend called me to the front of the line to do a solo. For the first time in a long time, I felt ALIVE, and I must have hogged that dance and done a solo that lasted most of the song. People stopped dancing and clapped for me the entire way through. I remember looking up and seeing my mom and brother clapping with more hope in their eyes than ever before. I remember wishing that moment would last forever because I had already decided that sometime very soon, I was going to end my life.

A little less than a half hour later, when I saw my parents getting ready to leave, I made it clear that I wanted to leave with them. I would usually be the last to leave any event and literally walk out of the hall simultaneously with the staff and cleaning crew.

As they began to say their goodbyes, I became even more anxious as I wanted to see very specific people for one last time. I wanted to hug them and tell them I'd missed them and was glad I got to see them. If one looked deep into my eyes, they could tell I was both sad and petrified. I wouldn't give them a chance to see my eyes long enough or ask me how I've been or when they will see me again.

Toward the end of my farewells, an old friend with whom I'd lost touch noticed something was off and asked me if I was OK. I started crying when she did, but I lied and told her not to worry, as it would soon "be OK."

Four days later, the events I described at the start of Chapter 1 occurred. This brings us to what happened after I told the paramedic, "You'll never understand me."

This was my first time in an ambulance, and I truly hope it was my last. The ride to the Royal Victoria Hospital emergency unit was likely no longer than fifteen minutes on the clock, but it felt like hours. When I finally got to the hospital, I was rolled in on the gurney and transferred to a bed in the hallway of the ER, where I stayed for hours, as there was no way a suicide attempt where the person clearly survived was going to take precedence over a "real" emergency.

I do not have actual evidence for this, and I'm not sure if it was the *monster* or my intuition that convinced me to believe this, but it very much seemed like I was unwelcome. I know a lot has changed these last few years, and there's still a lot of change needed, but twelve years ago, things were still deeply misunderstood.

At some point at night, a doctor came by to tell me my blood work results. Apparently, had I been brought any later to the hospital, I was on my way to serious liver failure. I had a hunch my situation wasn't great, judging by the troubled look on the triage nurse's face when she asked how long ago I had ingested 25,000 mg of Tylenol. In fact, I was immediately rushed into the ER hallway and injected with an antidote of some kind.

So, when that doctor came to see me in the wee hours to report my results, she told me that normal ACT levels in a liver shouldn't be higher than 36 U/L (I will spare you the medical details; a Google search on the topic gave me all I needed to know), and mine had reached 1000 U/L. Imagine if I hadn't thrown up shortly after ingesting all that Tylenol. Actually, don't imagine that. Imagine being told this news by a doctor with a judgmental look on her face. She was basically telling me how close I came to liver failure with an expression that said, "You're a f*ckin' idiot."

My brother stayed by my side for a couple of hours, and then Olga came by to hug me and tell me how much she loved me. She also said an old friend of mine, who I'd recently had a bullshit falling-out with, had come to the hospital with her, but he was waiting outside as he was too scared to come in. Visiting a friend hospitalized for a suicide attempt is uncomfortable because the conversation around all this has yet to be normalized.

A couple of hours after the doctor's visit, my mom appeared. This encounter was very different from the one we had about nine hours earlier when she and Tony showed up at the location of my attempted suicide. This time, she shook me. Yes, she literally grabbed me by the shoulders as I lay in the bed, yelled at me for about thirty seconds (which felt like a lot longer as I was drained as hell and mortified all in one), and then she left.

She showed me the magnitude of her shame and anger in a single minute. At that same minute, not only did I wish I had never turned on my cell phone when I did, but I also went as far as to wish I had never been born.

About ten hours after that, I was finally taken to a room (or more of a section blocked off by curtains) where I would remain until there was a room available in the psych ward. Again, everything I wanted to avoid by ending my life was going to come my way and come my way hard.

By evening, two other great friends came to visit at the same time, completely unplanned—Fotini, practically a sister, and my good friend Theo, who had assisted my brother the year before in his quest to find me a psychiatrist. There were many awkward silences during their visit; as I said earlier, visiting a friend who has tried to end their life is an uncommon occurrence for most people. And what made it even more awkward was what followed next. My brother walked in ... with ... my ... dad.

There he was, Johnny "Buymore" himself, staring at his pretty, broken daughter lying on a hospital bed the day after she tried to end her life. The man who moved to Canada in his late twenties worked harder than anyone I know to start his businesses. He continued to work harder than anyone I know (except my mom) to start a family and provide for them in abundance. There he was, looking more powerless than ever, a deep sadness on his face and tears in his eyes. Tears of sorrow as well as relief as he got to see with his own eyes that his little girl was still alive.

He put his hand on my ankle, looked into my eyes, let some of those tears roll down his face, and, in no time, disappeared behind the curtain that separated me from everyone else. My brother left to walk my dad to his car, and my two good friends bore witness to it—one of the most heartbreaking moments of my life.

It was embarrassing, to a certain extent, given the shame I already felt for what I had just put my family through. To top off the guilt and shame, my friend Theo inadvertently added to it when he leaned over me and said, "Did you see the look on his face?"

"Yes ..."

"Did you see all that pain?"

"Yes."

"Good. I hope that image of his face stays with you forever so that you will remember it the next time you decide to do something stupid! Because if you do this again, you WILL kill him."

At that moment, I wished I was already dead.

(Theo, I don't aim to make you feel bad when you read this. I know how hard nearly losing a friend to suicide could have been, and I know how heartbreaking it was for you to witness what you did. I know that twelve years later, you understand way more than you did back then, and I am beyond grateful that you broke through the discomfort of visiting me in the hospital and being present with me in a moment when most people wouldn't be, a moment where I needed someone I care about to be present. I'm grateful for your ongoing support ever since and grateful you helped me spread this movement and normalize the conversation!)

Moments later, my brother came through the curtain and joined another awkward silence. He was so uncomfortable that he displayed the most random excitement out of nowhere.

"Guess what?" he said.

"What?"

"Yesterday was 3:16 Day," he replied, referencing what many WWE fans consider Steve Austin Day.

At that point, I rolled my eyes and turned onto my side as if I cared what day it was when I tried to die. As if it mattered. As if we were growing up as wrestling fans and practically worshiping Stone Cold, Steve Austin, a.k.a. Austin 3:16, was even worth mentioning at a time like this. Ever since getting on Facebook in 2007, Tony would post on March 16 (3/16) in honor of Stone Cold Steve Austin. So that morning, he woke up and wrote a status saying, "It's 3:16 today! Those who know ... you know."

He did not yet know that 3:16 Day would take on a whole new meaning for him.

Chapter Six

The Decarie Expressway

IN THE DAYS THAT followed, I thought I was being transferred to the psychiatric unit, but there was still not a spot available. I was instead put in some kind of transition unit with a few others also in need of a psych spot and who had more severe illness than I did. I could hear them screaming at the top of their lungs from up and down the hall for five days.

I was heavily medicated, dressed in a hospital gown, and looked no more alive than a zombie. A few good friends visited and saw me in ways they never thought possible. I vividly recall how numb one of my best friends looked when he sat on the bed across from me and tried to process what the hell had happened. I am grateful to those who managed to pierce through that barrier of discomfort and visit me: Joe, Telly, Mary, Lenio, Stevy Z ... From the bottom of my heart, thank you.

Eventually, I was transferred to the Allan Memorial Institute of Psychiatry on the third floor. My level of self-loathing had reached an even higher level, and it was no secret that I had been counting the days to get back out and try again. Yes, despite all that had happened, and still running the risk of not "succeeding" with my next attempt, the *monster* was feeding my urge to try again.

A few hours later, a nurse came to my room to conduct an intake and asked me, "Do you still have thoughts of suicide?"

And I couldn't help but answer bluntly. "You seriously f*ckin' think I got over it already?"

This abrupt response stumped the nurse, who then asked me for further clarification. At that point, I made clear that I didn't love my life any more than I had the week before. Boy, was I in for a real treat following such an honest intake session?

An hour or so later, after having just spoken to my mom on the phone, a psych ward aide came to escort me from my room to another room with nothing more than a bottle of water and a magazine. Make no mistake—this new room wasn't an upgrade. This was an *isolation* room.

As if I didn't hate my existence enough, being secluded in a room with no window, away from any contact with anyone, really didn't help. My anxiety spiked, and although I hadn't considered harming myself while on the unit and was very much going to wait until I got out before attempting to end my life again, all that abruptly changed. To say I started freaking out is an understatement.

Minutes going by seemed like hours. I couldn't believe that I was being punished for being honest about how I felt regarding my life circumstances. I had never expressed that I had an intention or plan to attempt suicide over the coming days or while on the ward. Had I, that type of response would have merited further vigilance, possibly even as far as isolation if I demonstrated any physically aggressive behavior toward myself or others—but that was far from the case.

The sheets of my bed had been stripped for my own safety, as they are commonly used by suicidal folks in psych wards or prisons to hang themselves. So I sat there on my sheetless bed, unable to get comfortable, worried about how long I would have to live this way, worried about not being able to call my mom or my brother, worried about how they wouldn't know why I was no longer reaching out for them, worried about what else could happen to me at this point. All this worry fueled my anxiety and irrationality more and more.

After an hour or so of what felt like I was truly losing my mind, I fixated on the idea of ending my life in the psych ward, in that room, if possible. And yes, it was possible. Painful, no doubt, but possible. But what could I use to end my life in an isolation room designed for the prevention of such an act?

When you've reached that level of desperation and have already read everything available online about methods of ending your life, you find a way. From all the knowledge acquired during the depressive episodes I lived through, until this day, even if asked to do so, I can scan any room at any time and point out all the possible ways one can attempt to die and very likely succeed in doing so. That small royal-blue bottle cap, usually available on NAYA water bottles in

Quebec and other parts of Canada, became a potential object of suicide. My only way to go was to choke myself by swallowing it.

Since I have come this far in describing uncomfortable details from the times I attempted suicide, I figure this is a safe place to keep going. So yes, I tried to choke myself with this bottle cap, and clearly, I did not succeed. What I did succeed in doing was adding more to my traumatic experiences. Despite vomiting, I kept trying, using the same level of possessed determination I'd used while swallowing every tablet of Tylenol just a week prior.

At some point, I had to stop trying, as an aide came by to drop off a tray of food with plastic cutlery, which did not allow me to go eat in the dining area with the other patients. He noticed I had thrown up and assumed I was severely anxious. Within moments, he had come back to clean it up, and during that time, rather than simply eat my food, I assessed if there was any chance I could choke on something on my plate instead.

I momentarily gave up and allowed myself to eat because the medications I was on had tremendously increased my appetite. I told myself I would try again later, as it clearly didn't look like I was going anywhere for a while. I then decided to wait until the aide came for my tray so as not to risk getting interrupted or found too quickly after having choked, should I succeed this time.

Time passed slowly, and given how understaffed hospitals and psych wards were back then, being in the isolation room meant I was out of sight, out of mind. Luckily, enough time had elapsed from my entry into isolation to the time I'd been waiting for my tray to be picked up, and my mom and brother suspected something was wrong, given that I hadn't called.

They began to call, and at first, weren't given a straight answer as to why I could not come to the phone. Due to their persistence and determination to hear from me directly, eventually, they were told that I was put in isolation and was not allowed to receive or make phone calls. I later heard that my brother blew his top off on the poor soul answering the phone at the front desk.

My mom and brother were in a bit of a pickle at the store that day. It was a busy Monday, and two of their valuable staff members had called in sick. Neither of them could leave right away to come to see me, which frustrated them and compounded their angst. Eventually, they closed the store and showed up at the hospital.

I remember the petrified look on my mom's face when they let her in the isolation room to see me, and she found me sitting on the floor in the corner, looking pretty demented at that point. After she saw that nothing had happened to me, the aide took her out of the room and brought her to the living area to wait for me to be transferred back from isolation to my former room, which was already no longer available as someone else had been admitted to the ward that day.

At that point, my family and I wondered if I'd been put in isolation for my safety as initially told or out of temporary convenience. My brother then swore that he would do everything he could to get me out; I was in there not by our choice but rather per court order, given I'd attempted suicide the week prior.

Fun fact: The aide who put me in isolation (merely following orders from the nurse who had assessed me as a danger to myself) later became the person I looked forward to speaking to the most throughout my three-week stay. He was a huge Habs fan (the hockey team in Montreal), and I knew this because when we had the game on TV in the common living area, he would poke his head in as often as he could to catch a glimpse or ask for a score update.

Bedtime for all was before the game would be over, so since I didn't have access to my phone while on the ward, I would look forward to him telling me about it when he started his new shift the next night. Those little moments of positive connection with him were the tiny pockets of happiness I experienced during that time.

Less than four years later, in January 2015, I began working at a private addiction rehab in Montreal. Guess who the aide was during the day shift?

The psychiatrist on the ward, Dr. Theo Kolivakis, was pleasant to talk to and gave me significantly more time in our meetings than a psychiatrist had ever given me. I felt comfortable with him and relatively at peace in his presence. But the minute it was time for me to leave his office, my anxiety would rise.

It was evident to him that I didn't belong on the unit, that I was essentially being kept there for safety, and the treatment and assistance he heard me pleading for (again regarding my "intellectual disability") was not going to be found so long as I was still on the ward.

Eventually, I was given a pass to leave on weekends, the first weekend out having to return by 6:00 p.m., the second one being allowed to sleep in my own bed on a Saturday night and return by Sunday before bedtime. I had mixed emotions surrounding this pass. On the one hand, I was happy to get the hell out of there, but on the other, I felt guilt and shame around my family and whoever came by to visit my parents' home while I was out. I was also quite distressed upon returning to the ward. I thanked Dr. K. for allowing me these passes and would lie through my teeth when telling him I had no thoughts of harming myself while out there.

I was plotting every moment I wasn't talking with a family member. Heck, when I was quiet, and they were instead doing the talking, even then, I was plotting. I am not saying I fooled Dr. K. and that he actually believed everything I said; what I am saying, though, is that I spent a lot of energy trying to deceive him and others so that instead of being returned to isolation, I would be released into society so I could do it again—and get it right this time.

A month or so after the suicide attempt, I was finally released on the condition I would see a psychologist once a week and return for follow-up with Dr. Kolivakis on a weekly basis until further notice. And I did just that. I saw the psychologist he recommended. My brother made clear that we were willing to go down the private route, given I would otherwise be put on a long waiting list, and that we would be willing for me to see the psychologist twice a week in the beginning—anything to get me out, and anything to help me recover sooner rather than later.

While I did what Tony promised I would, during the day, I would spend a lot of time in my room fantasizing and reading about how I could make it work this time. At night, I would venture out to one of the overpasses of the Decarie Expressway in the very same Ford Escape I tried to end my life in. I parked my car at a different block almost every night, walked to the railing of one of the many overpass options along this highway, and visualized where I would have to jump from to succeed in killing myself. I had to ensure I wouldn't end up back at the Allan this time.

I kid you not; this happened practically every night for a little over two months. I would walk around near the overpass and look for parts that had less lighting so pedestrians or drivers wouldn't notice me hovering, waiting for the right moment to jump. I wouldn't be gone longer than an hour, not to alarm my family. I would often end my "visualization exercise" with a stop at either the McDonald's or Tim Hortons/Wendy's nearby and return with a shake or iced cappuccino to minimize their suspicion.

Little did I know that they had installed a tracking device under my car and would have found me in no time if I had not answered their call or gone "missing" for over an hour. Just as the saying goes, desperate times call for desperate measures.

To backtrack a little, before leaving Ottawa, in my despair, I had sought out a psychologist, Dr. Karen Ogston, who worked with children and adults with anxiety, depression, and behavioral and/or developmental difficulties. If it's not obvious by now, I chose her because of her expertise with people with *developmental* difficulties more than anything.

Truth be told, Dr. Ogston did the best she could to support me during my extreme depressive symptoms and throughout my insistence that my mental and learning challenges were so severe that I would never be able to make it in life. I know how badly I frustrated and discouraged a lot of the mental health professionals I saw nearly every week during most of the depressive episodes, including Karen, but she never gave up on me.

As daunting as I described my future, Dr. Ogston was relentless in helping me see that there's always hope. This was when she recommended that I read a book by a psychiatrist who was fascinated by how the brain can heal itself. The book was Dr. Norman Doidge's.

I couldn't believe she would recommend this book. "But I'm retarded.[1] I won't be able to read and understand this kind of book," I told her.

"If you find reading challenging, the book is also available in audio format. This should make things easier for you, Sophia. And there's no rush to get through the entire book. Just take your time."

"I'm slow. I have no choice but to take my time. Either way, this won't change anything. Retardation[11] doesn't go away!"

Or does it? About ninety brutal days following the above conversation, I finally decided to give this book a shot. There I was, lying in bed a couple of hours before my usual drive to the Decarie overpass. I was extremely bored, and I thought to myself that I had nothing to lose by listening to the audiobook I'd ordered on Amazon just a week or so prior. Imagine that—it took me a couple of months after Dr. Ogston recommended purchasing the book. Why? Because every day that followed that conversation was a day I thought I was going to manage to end my life—including the days before and after 3:16 Day of 2011.

---

1. See prologue

Even after being hospitalized for four weeks following the suicide attempt, and ESPECIALLY because I had been hospitalized, I truly wanted—or rather, the *monster* had me convinced that I truly wanted—to end my life, STAT.

So, I picked up my headphones and gave it a go. As I listened to the table of contents, I realized that Chapter 2 was absolutely the place I wanted to be. The title was "Building Herself a Better Brain—A Woman Labeled 'Retarded' Discovers How to Heal Herself."[2] I trust it is obvious by now why this title pulled me in. My heart actually started racing, and I skipped the introduction and Chapter 1 to listen as attentively as possible to what the author was about to tell me in Chapter 2—and boy, am I grateful I did.

The chapter introduces us to Barbara Arrowsmith Young, born in Toronto in the early '50s. She is the woman who built herself a better brain despite having several areas of cognitive delay. Despite these distressing challenges, Barbara made significant advancements in brain research that I am very grateful for today, as are many others across the globe.

This was the first I had ever heard about this extraordinary woman ... the first I was ever exposed to such an exceptional human being who did something so rare in the scientific community! How could this even be?

---

2. See prologue

Well, turns out "her brain was 'asymmetrical,' meaning that these exceptional abilities coexisted with areas of retardation."[3]

Hearing those last few words had me even more attentive than before I started, and I jolted upright. It described in great detail all the difficulties Barbara had experienced because of the areas of "retardation" in her brain. The author's description progressively moved on from major difficulties to *debilitating* difficulties. I was in shock and, oddly enough, grateful that I didn't have things anywhere near as bad as the *monster* had me convinced. That thought alone introduced a promising shift.

Imagine this: growing up, Barbara experienced difficulties with real-time understanding and had to review past events to make sense of them constantly. Unfortunately, this led her to face relationships and emotional development challenges. This further led to chronic doubt, uncertainty about everything, and feeling like she was living in a fog. Like many children with severe learning disabilities, she questioned her own sanity.

I invite you to pause for a moment and try to visualize such an experience for yourself. No, really—pause for a minute or two and get back to this chapter, the moment you've tried to fathom

---

3. *The Brain That Changes Itself: Stories of Personal Triumph from the Frontiers of Brain Science Paperback*. Dr. https://www.amazon.com/Norman-Doidge/e/B00J91097A/r ef=dp_byline_cont_book_1 . (December 18, 2007).

not understanding your life in real time and having to repeatedly question what you've just lived.

I hope you did pause because, honestly, most of us take way too many things for granted. I'll bet something like understanding what is going on in real-time is one of those things. There are too many events in our day-to-day functioning that we consider a given and, in turn, do not practice gratitude for. If we did, we would realize how much of an abundant life we already have and not walk around with this pervasive feeling of constant wanting, rarely having enough, rarely being enough, and craving more.

If you allow it to, your mind can continuously rob you of opportunities for happiness. FYI, there is actually a better way to live. If you really want it, I can show you strategies to make gratitude an integral part of your daily experience so you, too, can continuously reap the benefits of this natural and free stress buster!

Going back to what I was learning while listening to this exceptional audiobook, I found myself connecting with Barbara more and more. Dr. Doidge talked about how one day, during Barbara's graduate studies, a person who ran a clinic for kids with learning disabilities suggested a book by Aleksander Luria. At this clinic, practitioners used treatments based on the accepted theories and understanding of learning disabilities at the time.

This book by Luria describes a young Russian lieutenant injured during a WWII battle in May 1943. This man's injuries led to very odd symptoms that Barbara could relate to. When reading parts of this man's diary, she found that his experience very much described her own life. Luria had made sense of this man's problem, and Barbara realized, for the first time, that her cognitive deficit had a specific cause!

All of that sounds pretty amazing, but there was just one crucial problem: Luria's research did not offer a solution. The more aware Barbara became of the extent of her impairment, the more she felt overwhelmed and hopeless. The more she read about all this, the more she thought she could not continue living in this state, and as a result, "on subway platforms, she looked for a spot from which to jump for maximum impact."

Needless to say, when hearing that last sentence, I finally felt like someone else out there would understand me. Something I hadn't felt in a very long time and something that suddenly gave me HOPE.

At age twenty-eight, Barbara came across a paper by Mark Rosenzweig while she was in graduate school. I wish I could spare you the scientific details as I know not everyone is into those, but the details ahead are really key in understanding how this woman did the "impossible." From the University of California at Berkeley, Rosenzweig studied rats in different environments and found that brains in stimulating environments had more neurotransmitters, were heavier, and had better blood supply than those in nonstimulating environments. He demonstrated neuroplasticity by showing that activity could change the brain's structure. These findings inspired Barbara; she saw that the brain could be modified, giving her hope that compensation would not be the only solution.

As Dr. Doidge wrote, "[Barbara's] own breakthrough would be to link Rosenzweig's and Luria's research."

At that moment, I stood up. I started to pace in anticipation of what would come next. Did Barbara have the breakthrough she hoped for? The one I was desperately hoping for? What could she have come up with and done for there to be an entire chapter about her in this book?

Essentially, despite struggling with such brain impairments, Barbara isolated and dedicated herself to intense mental exercises in an attempt to overcome her OWN difficulties. Who does that?

As I said earlier, this was the first time I'd been exposed to such an exceptionally rare human being and scientist, and I hope it isn't the last in my lifetime. Instead of relying on help from others, she focused on exercises that challenged her weakest ability. As she improved, she added more complexities to the exercises. Eventually, Barbara saw improvements not only in her clock-reading skills but also in other areas, such as grammar, math, and logic. She also started to grasp what people were saying as they spoke, and finally, for the first time ever, she could live in real-time.

As if that weren't enough, she kept going and going, designing exercises for her other disabilities, such as her challenges with space, limb awareness, and visual impairments, eventually bringing them "up to average level."

And voilà, the power of hope was officially upon me!

In 1980, Barbara and her husband opened the Arrowsmith School in Toronto. After years of further research and development of her exercises, she discovered that individuals with learning difficulties often exhibit milder versions of cognitive impairments like those seen in Luria's patients. Children and adults applying to life-altering schools undergo extensive assessments lasting up to forty hours to identify their brain's weaknesses and determine if they can be improved. Before the narrator even finished talking about that last part, I grabbed my phone and texted my brother.

"Tony ... I am moving to Toronto!"

"What? You don't even want to leave your bedroom, and now, suddenly, you want to move to Toronto? What the f*ck?"

"Tony, I need you to come home. I need you to listen to this audiobook I just heard to make sure I understood correctly because I don't trust myself. Please ... just come."

"What audio is this? Why does this matter so much right now?"

"Because I think I finally found something that can help me. Something that can really change my life. And it sounds too good to be true. But if it is true, I need to move to Toronto."

"I'm on my way."

A little before sunset, my brother walked in, grabbed my headphones, and listened.

I nervously watched him, desperately hoping he would hear the same thing I had. A minute or so later, his face lit up, and he snatched the notepad and pen I had in front of me and started writing really fast. He was so focused and eager to write down everything he heard that it was as if his life depended on it, but it didn't—mine did.

"I'm not crazy, right? You're understanding the same thing I am?"

With hand gestures, he hushed me so he could continue listening carefully. About five minutes later, before finishing the entire chapter, Tony stood, walked out of my room, and ran down the stairs to our parents, who were sitting on the front porch.

"Sophie's moving to Toronto," he told them.

"What?"

"We found a solution for her, and that solution is in Toronto."

"What do you mean?"

"There's actually a program out there that can help her get rid of all her disabilities!"

My parents were confused, given over and over I had told them there was no "cure for retardation."[4] They also said there was no way I could survive on my own. They were also concerned about how this would work, given that I would have to live alone in Toronto.

I stood on the sidelines and watched my brother plead with them to give the OK on this. He was desperate to get his little sister help and had never felt this hopeful about anything in his entire life.

To be quite honest, neither had I.

Before I knew it, my brother had googled the Arrowsmith program and was on the phone with someone in charge at the school in Toronto.

Money appeared not to be an object—plus, my parents and my brother would likely have sold their souls to the devil if it meant saving my life. So when Tony told my parents that the program was $20,000, there wasn't a single objection. The problem was that his face changed color seconds later because he was told the program was full for September, and I would have to be put on a waiting list for at least a year.

"You don't understand. My sister might not last another year. She attempted suicide a couple of months ago and feels so hopeless that I don't think we will be as lucky the next time she tries something like

4. See prologue

this. There's gotta be a way we can move her up on the list. Something ... anything!"

Tony was told that the only other available adult program was in Vancouver unless I was willing to be in a mixed program with mostly children at their sister school in Peterborough, Ontario. Tony replied, "If getting to Vancouver is the only way, we will find a way. But please confirm as soon as possible if she can join the program in Peterborough."

I looked at my brother and fearfully said, "I wouldn't be able to make it on my own in Vancouver, Tony. I can't make it on my own here because I'm so challenged—how the hell would I make it on the other side of the country?"

"You don't know if Vancouver is where you'll have to go yet, so please relax. But if Vancouver is all we have, then Vancouver is, and I will move there with you."

Did I really need confirmation that my big brother loved me? Probably not, since he had demonstrated it quite a bit over the years as he helped raise me. But now, with what he was willing to do, he was more than proving it.

For the next hour or so, I patiently waited for my brother to receive the phone call from the director of the Arrowsmith School in Peterborough to determine whether there was space in their school or if he would need to pack up his entire life and move to Vancouver with me.

That was one of the longest hours of my life. Though I had shifted from wanting to plan my next suicide attempt actually to feeling the power of hope come over me, I still couldn't stop the guilt over the idea of my brother dropping everything to move to Vancouver.

The call came in, and my brother answered, putting the director on speaker. He explained my story, and she began to seek clarification ...

"Did you say your sister has already completed a master's degree?"

"Yes."

"So she has already gone to university, even reached the master's level, *and* completed the master's degree?"

"Yes."

"I must say that in the history of the Arrowsmith School, we have not had an adult sign up for our program after having already made it this far into their studies. I just want to make sure this is what your sister is looking for and that she would be a good fit for this program."

"Believe me, she is. She has struggled with school quite a bit throughout her adult life and keeps repeating to us lately that she would have never been able to graduate if it wasn't for us taking care of everything for her financially. She never had to work. She chose to do so in the summer, but not for survival purposes."

"I am baffled ... I am sorry to hear your sister has had such a difficult experience throughout her education. Her determination is remarkable, and I would really love to meet her."

"Determined, stubborn. Yeah, that's definitely Sophie. How soon can we meet to get this all started?"

"Testing for admission to the program takes place in Toronto over three to four days. The next week of testing will occur at the end of the month. Can you block off a few days to make it?"

"Just tell me when and where, and we WILL be there."

And there I was...

From beyond hopeless to beyond hopeful.

For the first time since it all began...

I no longer felt that no one understands me.

I no longer felt this intense level of helplessness.

I no longer felt the urge to jump over...

The Decarie Expressway.

Chapter Seven

"But What Did John 3:16 Really Say?"

SEPTEMBER 2011 ROLLED AROUND, and my mom helped me move to Peterborough, Ontario. We brought my stuff to The Village on Argyle, a private residence with students from all over the world and other young adults who attended the Arrowsmith program. In due time, friendships developed, and some felt like family, little brothers and sisters mostly, because at twenty-seven, I was the oldest student living there.

And so here it is. Here is how I began posting at 3:16.

One day, I proudly wore my Habs hockey jersey and sat in the common area on the first floor to catch a Habs versus Leafs game. A couple of my "little brothers" couldn't help but ask why I had "3:16" on my hockey jersey, and I explained that throughout the '90s, I watched wrestling with my big brother. Heck, in 1987, when I was just over three years old, my brother took me to the Montreal Forum to watch WrestleMania III on the big screen with the main event featuring WWF World Heavyweight Champion Hulk Hogan successfully defending his title against André the Giant! (Shout-out to my wrestling fans, who know what the hell I'm talking about!)

If you know anything about the WWF (today known as the WWE), you know that in 1996, at the June "King of the Ring" Tournament, the final round match was between Stone Cold Steve Austin and Jake "The Snake" Roberts. Now, a reverend, Roberts, has retired from wrestling to participate in this event. At the end of the match, Austin hit Roberts with his finishing move and won the match and the King of the Ring Tournament.

After the match, Austin mocked Roberts' -preacher during his coronation as King of the Ring by uttering a quote: *"You sit there, and you thump your Bible, and you say your prayers, and it doesn't get you anywhere! Talk about your Psalms, talk about John 3:16 ... Austin 3:16 says I just whipped your ass!"*

That unscripted moment was the birth of Austin 3:16, which turned into a movement on its own among fans in the wrestling world. From 1996 on, I used that number in my passwords, grad rings, hockey jerseys, and wherever I could put a number. In fact, my brother and I were so obsessed with the number that one day, when fresh concrete had been poured on the sidewalk in front of our driveway, my mom committed an act of vandalism. She took a small tree branch and inscribed our initials and the number *3:16* in the drying concrete. Yes, my mom did such a thing—little did I know then that this act made my mom a pillar in cementing the **3:16 Movement.**

After my "little brother" heard my 3:16 story, he asked, "What did John 3:16 really say?"

I said, "You know what? Good question!" And then I googled it.

The New International Version says, "For God so loved the world that he gave his one and only Son, that whoever believes in him shall not perish but have eternal life."

After reading the verse and realizing I had survived on 3/16 of that year, I was profoundly touched. I felt very much aligned with what the verse said as I immediately associated my survival with my belief in Jesus and that I was protected as such.

I remember the boys looking at me and wondering what had just happened. Given the look on my face and the change in my posture, there was an obvious shift in me. They stared (not so) patiently, waiting for me to share what I had just read. And I did.

The Habs game didn't matter anymore. All I could think about was that these two numbers had been such a big part of my life for the fifteen years before that moment, and I didn't have a clue about their real meaning. Clearly, I didn't have a clue yet about how much more meaningful they were about to become to many other people in the world.

I texted friends who were aware of what had happened on 3/16/2011, including the verse and what I had just realized. I didn't die that day for a reason, a pretty good one, it seemed, if you judge by the Movement that grew out of those two little numbers in the years that followed. The friends and family members I had messaged at that point were all Greek and, for the most part, also unaware of what that verse in the Bible was about because Bible verses are not highlighted in the Greek Orthodox tradition. Instead, entire passages are read and elaborated on during liturgy.

Following their replies and a couple of conversations, I resumed watching the hockey game, but this time, I was very uninterested in the outcome. In the last period, I grabbed the pen on the coffee table and started drawing 3:16 on my left wrist. I honestly don't know what compelled me to do that, but I did and started visualizing it as a tattoo.

Before heading to class the next morning, I called Mike's Tattoo Shop in Peterborough and made an appointment right after school. I got the tattoo, which today reminds me of how lucky and grateful I am to be alive.

After that, something else happened out of nowhere. I began sharing a Facebook status every other day at 3:16 p.m. We haven't had Twitter, Snapchat, or Instagram yet. I would write, "It's 3:16, and I'm having a great coffee," or "It's 3:16, and I'm stuck in traffic," or "It's 3:16, and I'm relishing this killer pizza slice." My brother and I, along with many wrestling fans in the world, used to post on Austin's 3:16 Day, but ever since 3/16/2011, that day has had a new meaning for my brother and me.

Before I get into how posting at 3:16 p.m. developed into way more, it's worthwhile to note what came out of my attendance at the Arrowsmith School. I know there will be at least one reader who has struggled with learning disabilities who might benefit from learning about my experience and the possibilities out there!

After undergoing the lengthy but fruitful assessment process, I was told that I would likely need to complete up to two years to maximize the program's offerings fully. We would need to reassess after the first year to determine if I would benefit from the second year of cognitive training.

Every day, I completed exercises to strengthen targeted areas of weaker brain function that were essentially the cause of my specific learning difficulties. Throughout this book, I have referred to my difficulties as disabilities, as this is the most commonly understood term for one's struggles with learning. The Arrowsmith School refers to learning disabilities as *learning difficulties*. The program deals with the root causes of a learning difficulty rather than just managing its symptoms.

Most people think that assistance for students with learning difficulties can only be offered through finding ways to work around their difficulties in the classroom (and inevitably in the workforce later on). In contrast, the Arrowsmith program seeks to identify each person's area of dysfunction and strengthen it. Ultimately, the program strengthens learning capacities in the areas of reading, writing, mathematics, comprehension, logical reasoning, visual and auditory memory, auditory processing, nonverbal learning, attention, and executive function. Auditory processing, comprehension, attention, and executive function were where I needed the most help.

When June 2012 rolled around, nine months after this program had begun and it was time for reevaluation, I already knew I had come a long way, even without needing to see the assessment results. Beyond the valuable changes I'd already noticed a couple of months in, by the end of the program, on one of the last school days, I experienced an emotional moment when I realized I was now able to do something I never had before in my life: I sat in the classroom during recess, a class with elementary school–aged children in the majority, and started reading a book among these very loud children who were holding multiple conversations around me and even occasionally screaming.

I don't even remember how this book wound up there or if I simply sat at a desk that already had a book on it, but the bottom line is that curiosity hit; I opened to a page, and I started reading.

Unlike every other time in my life when reading through anything with even the faintest noise was impossible, I suddenly was reading this page, understanding everything it said without having to read a line or a paragraph over and over. At the same time, the decibels in the room were pretty high.

I couldn't believe what was happening. I didn't need to reread the page to comprehend, but I found myself rereading it because I couldn't believe what was happening! Midway through my second time reading it, a tear rolled down one cheek, then another. What an incredible moment.

Honest to God, every difficult thing I had gone through in my life up until that point—from struggles in college and university to depressive episodes to a suicide attempt and all the accumulated trauma—everything that led to my experiencing that very moment was worth it. EVERYTHING.

Though I didn't believe I needed an assessment to tell me that my brain had changed, I still completed it. I had achieved significant gains despite having missed probably two months of school days due to trips back to Montreal for my brother's engagement and wedding and other obligations. It didn't appear that I would need to complete an extra year, but I was told I might benefit from a part-time year. I told them I would think about it, but when I realized the part-time program meant I would just need to attend a program a couple of hours a day on Tuesdays and Thursdays to work on one exercise for nine months, I respectfully declined this option.

I didn't much enjoy living in Peterborough, and any chance I got, I drove to Toronto on weekends or even to Montreal at least once a month since that four-and-a-half-hour drive was a piece of cake when it meant I was going back to my family, close friends, and a more vibrant city.

I really wanted to get on with my life and resume helping people. I had spent a good decade and a lot of blood, sweat, and tears working toward this. The time had come to live out my purpose.

On the day of graduation from Arrowsmith, I was pretty emotional and cried when I was called up to receive my certificate along with kids less than half my age. Because of the second major depressive episode, I'd been unable to graduate with the friends I'd made while completing my master's degree (I finished it in December 2010 rather than in June 2010 like the rest of them). Then, because of the nasty 2011 depressive episode, I missed graduation entirely.

So, here I was, a year or so after the ceremony I had missed, graduating with children from a program that had nothing to do with acquiring any marketable knowledge but rather a strengthened brain to help me thrive in the world ... and change it. The fact that I was part of this ceremony with children who had completed a few years in the Arrowsmith program and were off to live a better life while completing their elementary or high school years made it all the more special. I was so grateful they'd been granted this opportunity to skip the greater suffering in their futures and be at less risk of developing the type of mental health issues I'd struggled with for years.

Most of what I do is to prevent others from suffering, especially when it's completely self-created and unnecessary. Just knowing these children were going to suffer significantly less than I had to reach my level of education with learning difficulties (and the low self-esteem that came with it) filled me with gratitude. That graduation meant more than the master's ceremony I had missed.

I moved back to Montreal shortly after that day and got back into the groove of things throughout that summer, reconnecting with old friends and making new ones. It definitely felt good to be home, but it was also stressful as I had to readjust to living with my parents while figuring out my next career move. I studied in Ottawa, and notoriously, Quebec is known for making professionals' lives a living hell regarding the equivalency of their studies in the province. As such, getting a job as a counselor was not possible.

I looked into signing up for a three-year postgraduate program in marital family therapy (MFT), and this seemed like an excellent option, not only so I could be certified and licensed in Quebec but also to get an MFT certification in the US. However, it would have been very beneficial if I had read more about how this program works, specifically their favored approach toward providing couples counseling, because it was far from aligned with my counseling and coaching style.

Honestly, I didn't give this psychotherapeutic counseling style a real shot, as I got a job outside the field as an ambassador for Nespresso and became president of my folkloric dance troupe. My attention was certainly divided, and I enjoyed leading the dance group to greater endeavors, including planning a four-day dance conference and the group's first-ever performance in Greece. I also got quite a high from the challenge of selling Nespresso machines to the public before they became popular enough for people to buy them without a second thought.

Along the way, my supervisors in the MFT cohort realized this program wasn't for me, and I most certainly realized my energy and personality weren't for them. One really great thing that came out of that one and only year I completed (minus gained experience from counseling couples and accumulation of additional internship hours that would count toward my Quebec licensure) was meeting an awesome professor by the name of Tom Caplan.

Tom, who taught toward the end of my second semester, was pretty much the only professor I got along with and who liked my personality. Tom was a seasoned marital family therapist, social worker, psychotherapist, professor, supervisor, and author. I hope I didn't miss anything, but overall, he's a badass in the field. In addition to everything mentioned above, he founded the Montreal Anger Management Centre, for which he still serves as a consultant.

In one of my last classes in the program, Tom brought up a needs-related model he had developed that also worked well in the context of anger management. Discouraged by my experience in the program, I sighed and then whispered under my breath, "I miss anger management." I really did not intend for anyone to hear that or interrupt our class (we were a small group of nine). Still, because I was sitting at a round table relatively close to Tom, he heard me and immediately sought clarification.

"What do you mean, you miss anger management? Were you in an anger management group?"

"No, I co-facilitated a couple during my first internship and then ran my own group by my third internship back at the Elizabeth Fry Society of Ottawa."

"Is this something you would be interested in doing again?"

"Absolutely. I haven't familiarized myself with what's out there in Montreal, as I thought that since I'm not officially a counselor in this province, I wouldn't be eligible to apply, anyway."

"If you're working toward licensure, then you could work with me as your supervisor. Let's talk after class."

That, right there, was the reason I was meant to join this program, even for just a year.

I do want to point out that before running for president of my dance troupe, I had serious hesitation to do so. Having experienced what I had the year before, I lived with constant fear of developing depression again if I put too much on my plate.

I'd been transitioning back to life in Montreal, which was stressful on its own. Additionally, my dad had recently undergone a nine-hour open heart surgery, and I was the one taking him to all follow-ups during his recovery. This coincided with the start of the new MFT program, which was very different from my master's studies.

I recall voicing this at a dance group general assembly, and at the time, I had been told I needed not to worry as a separate committee would plan the dance conference, and I would simply need to oversee it. Planning a trip to Greece was very much not in the cards yet, especially not for an entire dance troupe to partake in several performances. Things did get heavier a lot quicker than anticipated, and combined with losing my job early into 2013 (Nespresso Canada had terminated its contract with the US company that hired me), being put on probation even for the first time in my life in the MFT program. My dad had a mild stroke while my brother was on vacation in Cuba, and I was officially overwhelmed by March.

In April, I felt myself burning out and actively chose to take a three- to four-week temporary leave from the group. That meant not attending dance practices or meetings of any kind nor responding to the high volume of emails.

I continued to solicit sponsors for our conference because I still derived some pleasure from the challenge, but that's as far as my involvement went for that month.

I also decided to preserve my energy and recuperate by deactivating Facebook. I didn't have Instagram yet, as the app didn't really gain popularity until later that year. Still, I did spend sufficient time on Facebook, mostly uploading photos and responding to comments.

That took up much of my time and energy, so I needed a break. I wasn't sure when I would return, but I truly wanted to learn to live without it.

After I deactivated the account, though, within a few days, an unexpected thing happened. A good friend texted me and asked, "Hey! It's 3:16 … What are you doing?"

I was surprised to see that it was, in fact, 3:16 p.m. when that message came in. It occurred to me that because I was no longer on Facebook, people weren't getting my 3:16 p.m. status updates. Something inside me shifted when I received that message, and I wondered how many other people had thought of me at that time.

To my surprise, more messages came in, including emails from those who didn't have my phone number. Imagine that! After receiving those messages and emails at 3:16 p.m., I knew something valuable was going to come out of this, and it would all start by letting people know why I posted at that time, as most of the Facebook contacts I had didn't have the slightest clue of where that came from.

It wasn't time, though … I needed to regroup, finish what I started with my dance troupe, and complete the first year of my program. It was time to straighten myself out career-wise and figure out my next steps, given that I knew deep down there was no way I was going to stick around and complete this graduate program, regardless of the outcome of my probation.

In early May 2013, I began seeing clients at the Montreal Anger Management Centre under Tom's supervision. I first facilitated an anger management group for men before I began one for women. Luckily, another female therapist had joined the team and would be able to take over my group for July, as I was scheduled to perform across Northern Greece with my dance group.

That trip was an incredible and exhausting experience for which I am very grateful, but I couldn't wait to get back and resume working toward building my career in Quebec.

Surprisingly enough, months after returning and successfully running my groups at the center, I was given the opportunity to work as an addictions counselor in the Dominican Republic at a brand-new private, resort-like rehab facility scheduled to open in late August 2014. There, I would receive training in addiction counseling from world-renowned addiction intervention, relapse, and recovery specialist Roland Williams.

I was at a point in my life where I wanted to gain more experience in different areas of counseling before determining the specialty where I wanted to settle. My dad's godson had passed away from a terrible overdose at the age of twenty-seven a month prior, which really affected me and sparked my interest in the addiction treatment area. The fact that I had a real itch for an opportunity to become more independent (a theme of concern in all the depressive episodes I had experienced) also contributed to the ease with which I was able to accept this six-month contract that had the potential to grow into something greater.

A couple of weeks later, though, my best friend Mike and I came clean about how we felt about each other, and we decided to give us a shot. He knew I had accepted the opportunity, signed this contract, and would be leaving in about nine months, yet he still wanted to give us a shot as he strongly believed we would find a way to make it work.

A few days after Mike and I started dating, my dad's body didn't respond well to his blood thinners, and he fainted. We rushed him to the hospital. A couple of days after that, when my dad's health was back on track, we cut a cake for my thirtieth birthday in his hospital room. I was leaving my twenties behind and looking forward to better experiences throughout the next decade.

When 2014 rolled around, I continued to run groups at the Montreal Anger Management Centre and offer individual counseling under Tom's supervision at the Caplan Therapy Centre. I also continued to complete the courses required to get licensed in Quebec and worked on the website and marketing materials for the rehab center where I would be working in the Caribbean.

I also deepened my relationship with Mike, making it harder to anticipate my departure from the Dominican Republic. I believe these things played out in how they helped me endure the unbearable experience of being away from Mike as I realized how much I wanted to spend the rest of my life with him. The night he drove me to the airport, I was practically hyperventilating from crying.

Three weeks later, I was back in Montreal. Why? Because this opportunity was a bust, and the rehab center was far from ready to operate. Rather than management informing us of this, I and several other counselors arrived as initially scheduled, only to waste time watching people complete the project at an alarmingly slow pace. The only good thing that came out of those three weeks was the training I received from Roland Williams, and I will forever be grateful for that!

When I returned to Montreal and informed Roland that I would not be working at the center in the future, he offered me a huge discount on his Four-Day Relapse Prevention Training scheduled in Santa Monica at the end of the following month. I really enjoyed learning from him and wanted to make this work—and I did! Determination is part of my genetic makeup, and there was no way I would miss this.

What an incredible experience! This was my first time in California. The weather was remarkable on October 31, and the training took place at the Grammy Recording Studio in Santa Monica. That last part, on its own, was surreal. That very same night, I went to the annual West Hollywood Halloween Carnival, and the following night, I went to a dance featuring Cretan musicians—good friends of mine who happened to be in town at the same time!

The training itself was amazingly practical. I learned so much and developed such great connections as a lot of group work took place throughout. I was given a chance to shine, and unlike what I'd experienced in the MFT program the year before, people were amazed at what I had to offer, and I didn't need to tone down anything about my personality. Only two of us didn't have a history of addiction, but having a master's in counseling and having recovered from depression several times granted me respect from even the skeptics.

During a discussion with the entire group of attendees, one of the participants went as far as to say I triggered her. She repeated it and shared how uncomfortable she felt because of my presence. The way I validated what she felt and recognized her need helped her identify the thought trap that led her to believe what she did and led her to change her mind about me and want to work together throughout the rest of the workshop. Everyone witnessed this and other moments when I didn't hesitate to show vulnerability and use self-disclosure to benefit a potential client (while we practiced). Most were impressed with what I could do and got over the idea of my not having struggled with addiction. "It takes one to know one and to help one truly" suddenly became a thing of the past with a lot of the people there, and I was proud of myself for having been able to achieve that during the four-day workshop.

I returned to Montreal on a mission to put my valuable training into practice and find work in addiction treatment. While I looked for work, I encountered difficulties I never expected. Having a master's degree and the type of training I had overqualified me for the majority of addiction counseling jobs in Quebec. I received rejection after rejection because of this, and one day, while discouraged, I found myself distracted and staring at the tattoo on my wrist. I thought to myself, *I have been through much worse in my life—3/16/2011, and the last depressive episode definitely being worse than this.*

Suddenly, I remembered how much my Facebook and Instagram followers associated me with 3:16 p.m. on their clocks or cell phones. I also remembered how inspired a lot of folks felt during the training in Los Angeles upon hearing my story. Quebec rehabs didn't want my help? Quebec made it harder and harder for me to obtain a permit to practice psychotherapy. Well, too bad for Quebec. I was going to find a way to help people one way or the other and way beyond the borders of Quebec.

What better way to do so than by starting to do something that didn't require a license, permit, or any of my qualifications? What better way than by sharing my story and impacting people's lives by being authentic? Why not have people pause at 3:16 p.m. and think of something other than what I'm doing and think of what *they* are grateful to be doing at the moment instead?

Ideas poured through, and when my brother walked into the basement, I shared everything I envisioned doing. I remember him really liking my idea and telling me he wanted in whenever I got the ball rolling!

Chapter Eight

What Tony Has to Say About the Original 3:16 Day

SHORTLY AFTER LAUNCHING THE presale of this book, I made the first chapter available for free to the public.

I received great feedback that inspired me to keep writing and to keep going with my mission.

Even though I had intended to interview my brother regarding his experience, it was refreshing to see how many people wanted to know more about his experience on 3:16 Day. Some wanted to hear more from my mom as well, but I knew that would have to come at a later date, as there is still a lot of healing that needs to take place before we can interview my mom.

I knew my brother would be up for the task as he always told me he was ready to go all in when the time came to take the **3:16 Movement** further, so I didn't hesitate to organize an interview with him.

Sophia: Thank you, big brother, for being here with me today and allowing me to interview you. I know a lot of people would benefit from hearing about your experience as someone dealing with and caregiving for a loved one with depression. I'm going

to ask you a couple of questions about your experience on March 16, 2011, and the days that followed. I'll start by asking if there's anything you'd like to add or elaborate on from what I've already shared in the free version of Chapter 1.

Tony: Let's go back to the day itself, starting from that morning. I was expecting you at noon at the store.

Sophia: I remember.

Tony: On that day, you hadn't shown up by 12:15, and I hadn't noticed that you weren't there yet. Mom remarked and started calling you. You weren't answering. Then, by 12:45, she said she had been trying to reach you. Then I tried, and you still were not answering. I kept trying you every ten to fifteen minutes between dealing with clients, and at that point, I was getting progressively more worried.

By two o'clock, I called the police to file a missing person's report. When the police came, I tried to explain what we thought was going on. Then I started searching through my emails, looking for the distressed emails you'd sent me prior to that day. I showed the police officer one of your more recent emails as evidence that you're really in distress. After they read that email, they took things more seriously. They filed the report and left.

At that point, I was scrambling, trying to figure out where you could be. This time, I started calling around to some of our friends, Don Stefano being one of them. Right away, he showed up at the house, and we started splitting territory. We then went for a drive together, trying to think of where we could look. At one point, so aimlessly driving, we wound up on the mountain.

We came back down the mountain and tried to think. We then went home and continued to think of potential places you could be. After I mentioned a potential spot, he'd say, "Done," and get back in his car to look for you around that area.

At this point, word had gotten out through Mom, so our cousins started calling me, and other people were calling me back to whom I'd made a few calls or sent texts. Actually, I remember when I was in the car with Don Stefano, we called New York. We called Eleni to see if you had reached out to her and were in your car and on your way there, but she had not heard from you. She swore she hadn't heard from you, or else she would have told me. I was like, "Please don't keep it from me. I just need to know that she's safe." And she's like, "No, I really haven't heard anything." She asked me to please text her back if I had any news later.

Later, though, everybody was texting back at that point, as a massive citywide search party had begun. That evening, while we were driving around searching, our relatives gathered back at the house. It was a very morbid scene. They were crying in panic. It felt like coming home to a gathering relatives have when they just found out someone has died. Watching them all cry really felt like the precursor to your funeral. Mom was crying so much ... it's as if you were gone already. During all that, there was Dad sitting in a corner, not a word coming out of him ...

Sophia: How did that feel? Seeing that?

Tony: F*cking horrible. I just wanted to yell at everybody to calm the f*ck down. I told them a little more gently, but seeing all these people on a downer or whatever brings you down. It was a really morbid feeling walking into the house as if it was too late to save you. You were already gone.

We didn't walk into a search party ... we walked into a postmortem. And I really didn't have time to deal with all of them because I was still on the phone calling everywhere I could imagine.

I don't remember what time this was exactly—it was still evening—I stepped outside to get on the phone with Sandra, and suddenly, the other line started beeping, and it was you! And I just yelled out, "OH MY GOD, it's her." I didn't even say bye to Sandra. I just hung up and answered your call. I was like, "Where are you? Where are you?" And it's as if Mother heard me or was standing in the vestibule or something—bottom line, she heard me, and there was a commotion as I ran back in to grab my keys. At this point, I was signaling that it was you on the phone, and I needed to run to the car. You were trying to explain to me where you were, but you were groggy and wobbly in what you were saying.

I was too busy holding the phone. Holding the keys, trying to start the car ... I was scared of dropping the phone or something before finding out where you were. Mother followed me and had only her phone when she got in the car. I think she was even wearing house slippers out in the snow. It's like she saw that I was in such a rush and not going to wait for anybody; she just ran and got in the passenger seat. I didn't want her to get in the car with me, but she got in, and I started driving. Now that I had you on the phone, you were trying to explain to me where you were. She was freaking panicking. I even yelled at her at one point, "Stop panicking! F*ck, this isn't helping! Do you have your phone with you?" She did, so I told her to call 911.

So she did. I remember I had an iPhone, but she still had one of those old-fashioned phones and couldn't get it on speaker. I had you on speaker so that I could keep driving. Then I passed my phone to Mom and put hers to my ear to talk to the 911 operator. I was telling the operator what you were telling me and where you were more or less until you finally wobbled to the street corner to tell me that you were on the corner of St. Dominique and Marie-Anne. I repeated that to the operator, and by the time we got there, the cops were already there—and who were they? The ones who came earlier in the day to take our report. One of them grabbed my arm and told me you were OK, but I had to see with my own eyes.

I remember getting past him and poking my head in the car to check on you. I was so relieved to see you were alive. Mother was freaking out and crying, and I saw her push through and talk to you, but it wasn't until reading your first chapter that I knew what exactly she said to you. I just remembered her freaking out while we waited for the ambulance while her practically bare feet were in the snow.

Sophia: Wow ... I'll be honest ... hearing these extra details is informative, yet it makes my stomach uneasy as I have been reliving that day more and more since writing the chapter. I take it this isn't easy for you to recount, either.

Tony: No, it's not. But I am willing to keep going if you're up for it.

Sophia: I am.

Tony: Great, let's do this. The ambulance did not take too long to arrive, and for some reason... it honestly escapes me right now... they wouldn't let us in the ambulance with you. They said they would take you to the Royal Vic, so we drove there and even got there slightly before them. Olga got there shortly after we arrived, as she was the first person I texted after seeing for myself that you were OK.

I remember telling Mom to take my car and go home, which she fought with me about at first. But eventually, she realized there was nothing she could do in the waiting room and that it was best if she went to Dad. So she left, and I stayed and waited until they would let me see you again.

It was a hectic evening. They had you in some hallway in the emergency section, and when I saw there were a couple of rowdy drunks and drug addicts also waiting to be seen in that hallway, there was no way I was leaving you alone. I spent the night with you until 5:00 a.m. when Mom showed up. That was the first time I had to leave your side as two people weren't allowed in at once. I didn't sleep a wink that night because if anybody needed sleep, you needed it more than anything. I was hyper-vigilant at that point, aiming to protect you from any of the sketchy people I noticed walking near or toward you.

Sophia: I had forgotten about that. I also didn't know about that pre-funeral scene that took place at our home. Ever since you described that scene, my stomach has been upside down.

I have so many other questions regarding the details of that day, but the purpose of this interview isn't so much to get caught up in those details as it is to get a sense of what that day felt like for you.

Ultimately, there are two purposes for this book. One is to normalize the conversation regarding depression so that people now and in the future do not suffer in silence and openly speak of whatever distress they may be experiencing that's affecting their mental health. The second purpose is to help open people's eyes to what this *monster* ultimately does to the family, friends, and caregivers of those suffering from depression.

Someone could be reading this book right now who is also experiencing depression, not necessarily at the level described throughout this book, but enough to have had thoughts of suicide. If you're someone who has been told by this *monster* that your family and friends would be better off without you,

I want you to know that, ultimately, this is what a family really goes through when you listen to the *monster*.

If you've been convinced that the family will be better off without you, know that exactly the opposite will happen. The *monster* has a funny way of making you think this will be a walk in the park for them, but the *monster* is lying. I promise.

Someone else could be reading this book who's never experienced depression and who is not actively taking steps to improve or protect their mental health, who is letting stress overtake their lives. A person who is burning out and still not considering taking care of themselves, a person who may not love themselves enough actually to take preventive steps to keep their mental health intact, but who at least loves their significant others and their family members enough to do so. I hope that by interviewing you, Tony, and giving us a real sense of what this was like for you, the person who wouldn't normally invest in their mental health will see that this is what they may eventually put their brother, mom, girlfriend, or wife through. If you're that person reading this right now, consider taking better care of your mental health and working toward reducing your stress, letting go of the anger and resentment you've bottled up for some time, or even working on methods to improve your sleep habits. If you aren't willing to do this for yourself, do this for the people you love and love you back

because what Tony has been describing is what they might go through.

Bringing it back to you, Tony, I know that sharing about all these years later can't be easy ... and again, I am very grateful for you wanting to contribute to furthering people's understanding about what it's really like. Would you recommend to someone that they take better care of themselves so that they don't put their family through such a living nightmare?

Tony: Obviously, I can't stress that enough ... Because truth be told, in certain respects, I was lucky ... and so were you.

Sophia: What do you mean?

Tony: Well, through your various episodes, especially this specific one we've been talking about, I took three months off work because I was home taking care of you, pretty much making sure you wouldn't harm yourself. You essentially had to be on a sort of suicide watch after coming out of the psych ward.

We were privileged that I could take off work because we owned our own business, and at the time, Mom and Dad weren't as old and still in a position to take care of things without me.

But it was draining. I'd much rather have been at work. It was frustrating. It would make me angry because I couldn't get through to you. You know, going back to the actual day itself, coming home, and finding everybody in that morbid state, already crying as if a funeral was coming, that sucks the life out of a person. That day sucked the life out of me.

So had some of the days before then and after because of the damage you did to our parents and how you sucked the life out of them too. It was heartbreaking and draining to watch them constantly sit and cry—even "almighty" Dad, the man who never showed emotions.

It would start off with Mom being a total wreck, which would then bring down Dad, of course. They did whatever they needed to do at work, and then they were just in the office, sitting on their desk chairs, both pretty helpless and hopeless. And this went on for months. It started when we brought you back from Ottawa months after your hospitalization and until you discovered the Arrowsmith program.

I had no time to sit there and be depressed and sad for you. Everybody else was sad all around me. I had no time to deal with anything I was feeling. I had to take care of business. I had to take care of you. I didn't have the luxury to feel sad. I would feel anger as I watched THEM be sad. It angers me that they just couldn't snap out of it and be strong along with me.

Then, more anger would come. I'd be angry with you because you put them in this state, even though you didn't want to. I'd have anger toward you because I would try to talk to you, and it didn't matter what we told you; you would have a counterargument, or you wouldn't care. It didn't matter how logical or how much what I told you made sense; you would not listen. You just didn't care ... And that would obviously be frustrating. I went through a lot of anger and frustration, more than anything, which was mentally exhausting.

But I never stopped wanting to help you because you're my sister, and I love you.

Sophia: Can I interrupt you for one second? I am not going to lie; some of my unhealed trauma is coming to the fore, and I find myself feeling guilty, which I know consciously serves no purpose, but at a subconscious level, other things continue to happen. My neck has been tensing up like you can't believe, and I need to clarify something.

Now that you've read my first chapter, and you've heard me mention before, and as I do throughout this book, that depression is a *monster*—now that you've read me saying how much this *monster* was fueling my desire to end my life and that this monster was trying to convince me that you guys would be better off without me, that it pervaded my thoughts and led me to zero in on specific things I never would have in a right state of mind—from your experience, as someone who knows me well and how I am, knowing what a caring individual I usually am and then hearing me say "I don't care"... Knowing what you knew about me and then seeing me speak in the way I did, and behave the way I did, did it ever give you the impression that someone else had taken over?

Tony: Oh, yeah. I knew where you were going with this before you even finished your last sentence. You had pulled a complete 180. From alive, bubbly, loud, the life of the party, with a glow in your eyes, a smile that would light up any room, and a contagious laugh that could wake the dead, we were suddenly exposed to the complete opposite of your good qualities and traits.

It wasn't just the experience of talking to you and you not caring or listening that was draining. Practically everything that would come out of your mouth had us like, "What the f*ck? Where's this coming from?"

That just added to my frustration and exhaustion. I was so discouraged and depleted. I could no longer enjoy any hobbies because how could I enjoy anything, knowing what my sister was going through? How could I attend parties or events I was invited to—how could I?

You could say I was probably experiencing symptoms of depression at that point because of how helpless I felt.

Sophia: I saw that you were burning out. That's definitely safe to say. Burnout symptoms are similar to mild depressive symptoms, and very often, I tell people to take care of themselves when they feel like they're burning out to prevent depression because there's a fine line between the two, and when you cross over to the other side, it's a lot more life-threatening and a lot harder to recover from.

Whatever the case may be, you were definitely burning out, and with all the descriptors you've given about how energy-sucking the experience was and how fatigued you were ... it's safe to say that you were experiencing caregiver burnout. That's a real thing. So is caregiver depression. Maybe you never made it to caregiver depression because you weren't allowing yourself even to experience certain feelings for my survival, really, because if you didn't do what you were doing for me, then I don't know if I would have survived. Not because our parents didn't care for me but because of language barriers and whatnot. They couldn't have understood all that you did in the appointments you took me to and with all those professionals you've spoken to throughout these past twenty years since the first depressive episode.

Tony: Yeah ... and we could probably talk about this for a very long time, regarding all your episodes, but right now, I am really trying to convey the message that depression affects every family member.

You know, Mom can't give you an interview right now, but I can tell you at least a little of the effect that your 2011 depression had on her. It was truly heartbreaking to see Mom during that time. At that point, she no longer cared for anything or anyone but you, obviously. If something happened to you, it would have been the end of her life as well. I think she would have committed suicide following you and not even thought about me or Dad. That's the effect it had on her.

She lost her wits. She was no longer the person we knew. She was constantly crying. This *monster* sucked the life out of her.

I can't find the words to do any of this justice for people to truly understand how important it is not to let their mental health get to that point.

Sophia: Thank you for this, Tony. I know it's hard to find the words, especially when we are aiming to get this message out to people who've never experienced depression.

The theme throughout this book is that *Depression DOESN'T Discriminate*, so I really hope to get through to the person who thinks they're immune to depression and who is just carrying on burning out or adding even more pressure to themselves. Especially to those living in the pressure cooker known as North America.

This message is really for the person not taking steps to check in with themselves, not taking steps to listen to their needs, not taking steps to love themselves, and not letting go of anger. If you're one of those people and you're not willing to take preventive measures for yourself, then do it for the ones you love because, holy sh*t, do they ever go through a debilitating experience themselves!

Once you're depressed, you don't care much. It's like my capacity to feel love was lost. I can't explain it, but I love you

guys so damn much, and I couldn't feel love for anyone or anything at that point.

Tony: I recall. It didn't matter what we were going through. You didn't care, and you were so convinced that ending your life would put an end to your suffering and that we would no longer feel burdened.

When you were depressed, it didn't matter to you what we were going through. Or if it ever did, it was for a very short moment. You didn't care what damage was done to any relative. It's as if you were forbidden to care.

I wish I had the words. As educated as I am, I can't find the words to help someone really understand. I wish I had the words to make them understand what I couldn't even make you understand.

If you're burning out, please think twice before you push further through your burnout. Once you get deeper into it and become depressed, there's practically no turning back if you don't have a good support network and the right treatment.

You had me by your side, but unfortunately, others don't. I didn't have a wife and daughter at the time of that episode. Other people may also have a close sibling, but if that sibling is married with their own kids, they won't have as much time to spend as I did with you. Definitely not because they don't care, but because their lives are much more demanding.

Sophia: Everything you're saying about not having the words makes sense. A healer once told me that depression belongs to another dimension, and that is why, in this dimension, we don't have the words to describe what this experience is like properly.

That resonated with me. Just the idea that it's from another dimension, and that's why we cannot find the words in this dimension to express what it's really like, brought some peace at that point.

Even though I have lived with major depression four times, I still can't find the words to give you an accurate representation of this *monster*, as it belongs to another dimension.

Tony: I hope my words have been enough to describe my experience as a caregiver ... to at least help the family members of those who are going through it know that they are not alone and that there is support for them out there. If they ever seek me out online or in person and want to talk more about this, I'm there for absolutely anybody.

Sophia: Thanks, T. I am grateful for how much you want to contribute to this Movement and help people.

Earlier, when I asked you if you felt at any point that someone or something else had taken over my mind, you said, "Yeah, obviously." I hope that brings solace to caregivers and others who have loved ones experiencing depression because then,

hopefully, they'll realize that this isn't personal. Ultimately, the person suffering from depression isn't doing this on purpose and isn't actively trying to hurt their feelings and drain the hell out of them. It is like something else has taken over!

Tony: Yes. I can indeed attest to that. It was not you. You were taken over. Whether it was something from another dimension or whatever you want to call it, that was not you. That was not anything like you. Some of the anger and hate that came out of you in that state ... wow, was that ever nothing like you. It's like you were not my sister anymore, even though you were.

Whether you've bought this book because you want to support me, or you're someone who has known someone who's taken their life and can't quite wrap your head around it, or you've had a colleague who had to leave work due to depression and has kind of left you in a pickle in the meantime—whoever you may be, without trying to scare you, I want you to know that it can happen to you too.

I hope this opens your eyes to realize that if you don't take active steps to improve your mental health—or, as I often call it, emotional wealth—then it can happen to you, too.

People are driven to acquire financial wealth but do not realize that it is pointless without emotional wealth. I want people to realize that without emotional wealth, without taking steps toward acquiring emotional wealth and protecting their mental health, they could end up really turning things upside down for everyone else in their life.

Because that's really what happened here—I messed things up for the people I love. If you don't want to mess things up for the people you love, remember that **Depression DOESN'T Discriminate**, and it is really worth it for you to take the right steps to protect your mental health and make sure you don't burn out or cross over into depression.

Chapter Nine
When History Repeats Itself

WHEN 2015 ROLLED AROUND, the year started off with me still being considered overqualified for the jobs I applied for. But on Friday, January 9, things took a turn for the better when I got an email from a private rehab facility asking if I could come in for an interview the next week. I was so happy and grateful to receive that email; I felt in my gut that I would get this job! I had been emailing them since November, and we'd had a bit of a back-and-forth. Then, I heard nothing from early December on, so I gave up on the idea of working at this beautiful facility or in a rehab anywhere in the province of Quebec.

It boggled my mind how many people in Los Angeles and Orange County were ready to hire me after meeting me and seeing firsthand what I could do during the Four-Day Relapse Prevention Counselling Training I'd attended in October 2014. If I hadn't been dating Mike and hadn't already had a hard time being away from him when I worked in the Dominican Republic, I would've been on the first flight to California the second I received the emails from those facilities interested in hiring me.

I'm not gonna lie—there were moments when I considered pausing our relationship so I could spread my wings and fly, but I'm grateful that I was a little more patient and stuck around to receive that email when I did, as I don't know if I would have been this blessed as I am with Mike in my life.

Needless to say, I got the job. I was so grateful to be given the opportunity to make a difference and put into practice what I had learned in all my years of training. I created different six-week programs and directly saw their benefits while running a couple of weekly group sessions at the center (I have since recorded sessions and made them available to the public in the **"Prosper Through Emotional Wealth"** program at www.alive316.com). Everything I teach in a group coaching format to residents suffering from addiction and a comorbid mental illness, such as depression or even a personality disorder, is beneficial to anyone and everyone!

In most rehab and counseling facilities in Quebec, burnout rates are high because there's usually a staff shortage, and the workload becomes very demanding and draining. Although I worked in a private facility, it was still in its infancy and not overstaffed by any stretch.

Working in addiction is tough, but in this case, it was even tougher because the criteria for admission to this specific rehab entailed having a comorbid psychiatric disorder. This means the patient would need to have primarily an addiction along with another mental illness. This automatically stepped up the challenge of working in a rehab, which I gladly accepted at first. My self-care game wasn't top-notch then, so that didn't help, and my wanting to prove myself and get further in this field also didn't work to my advantage.

At around the six-month mark, a recruiter from an employee assistance company where I had once applied for an addiction counseling position reached out about a contract opportunity for me to offer consulting and counseling as an affiliate to their company. Essentially, I wouldn't be working for the company; they would just refer clients to me, and I could accept or reject the referral as I pleased. All I needed was an office to hold sessions in. Luckily, my manager at the rehab approved that during the time I was not seeing clients from the center, I would be able to see the clients referred to me as part of the employee assistance program (EAP).

This allowed me to gain experience in another area of counseling and offer services in a more short-term format, using a solution-focused psychotherapeutic approach, which I had liked very much during my graduate studies and hadn't been given the opportunity to apply since graduating.

Given that I felt myself burning out, I started subconsciously looking for an exit from the rehab center, and that's probably why I was ecstatic to hear from the recruiter of the other company, no matter how part-time the offer was. By the seventh month, however, I started developing headaches more often and realized that for both my physical and mental health, I would have to call it quits at the rehab center, so I did.

I gave a six-week notice of my departure, which is a long time for someone feeling physically and often mentally unwell. Still, when I knew my stay there was going to be temporary, a huge weight came off my shoulders, leading to a decrease in my headaches and sleep disturbance.

In the meantime, I looked into options for continuing to see clients referred to me from the EAP contract. I saw them there until the day I left the rehab. Then, following this, I began renting hourly space at the Caplan Therapy Centre and occasionally at my friend's counseling office downtown when he wasn't seeing clients.

This plan worked out, but I knew I wanted more. I wanted to decorate my office space, as I had at the rehab center, giving off the vibe I preferred. I believed the environment I was working in affected how I helped my clients, so not long after, I began looking for my own office to officially go full swing into private practice.

I fell in love with the first place I landed on, which was the basement of an old home in Westmount. There were several other doctors, psychiatrists, and psychologists in the building, just as there were other professionals in the adjacent buildings (also old homes) on Sherbrooke Street, right across from Westmount Park. The furniture consisted of unique vintage and antique pieces that were very much my style, and I visualized hosting my clients the way I would host someone in my own home, with warmth and comfort.

I immediately said yes, comfortable that I would be able to make the rent, even with just the current clients I had from the contract, with the plan to build slowly from there.

Within ten days, I secured two more contracts and then hired someone to start building my website so I could work on getting my own clients outside of the EAP contract referrals. Part of the reason for this was that as much as those contracts were a blessing for getting me started on building my own practice, the hourly rate was nowhere near what my work was worth. We would get paid up to forty-five business days after completing the sessions the clients had been allocated. Again, this is a great way to start but not a great way to maintain a steady income.

By October 10, I had my first office warming with family and relatives, as my office was big enough to fit about fifteen people. I could easily run counseling groups in a circle of up to ten, another reason I was so compelled to say yes when I saw the office. A couple of days later, I also held an office-warming party with friends. I was grateful for them having been there for me throughout the depressive episodes and for their support. We raised a glass of bubbly in my office and then went back to my parent's place for a lovely Momma Manarolis feast.

I was really excited for what was coming. I had recently attended a life coaching training. I was excited to start including life coaching in my menu of services, as I'd noticed people were becoming more and more open to seeing a coach over a therapist.

I was grateful that I could offer both counseling and coaching and for the endless possibilities that lay before me, especially after the experience I'd gained running groups in and out of the rehab center. I had the space to run groups and workshops, and the office location itself added a bit of prestige, allowing me to attract a clientele willing to pay me what I was worth.

All seemed well with the world and the direction I was headed in, minus how easily I could get distracted by my other passions, such as dancing with my troupe. An opportunity to perform on a TV show in Greece in the following month presented itself, and I couldn't help but say yes, pausing my professional momentum. It was not one of my wisest decisions (the TV show experience was really nothing to write home about), but overall, I enjoyed being in Greece in the fall. It allowed me to spend time with relatives who are typically unable to hang out during the busy high-summer season. They hadn't seen me since the summer of 2013 and wondered if my dating Mike had anything to do with it. I assured them it didn't, that it mostly had to do with adulting and building my career.

Then 2016 started off with a proposal in the middle of Las Vegas Boulevard while fireworks shot from the rooftops of five different hotels on the Strip, as the countdown for the New Year had just taken place. This is the kind of note on which the year began, with tears of joy and laughter, when I eventually said yes to Mike, asking me to marry him.

The goal had initially been to hit the ground running as soon as 2016 started, to get my counseling and coaching business to the level I had anticipated before pausing the month before. I wanted to further my training as a coach and offer my services virtually to people in different parts of the world. I wanted to network in Westmount and attend any event I could, to have conversations with the right people and get more clients; as a result, the kind who would pay me then and there and not forty-five days later—the kind who were willing to invest in their personal development and enrichment.

Planning an engagement and a wedding and looking for a place to live were far from my 2016 radar when I'd set my annual goals. Since I'm five years older than Mike, he still had some of the things he wanted to accomplish, so I didn't expect a proposal that early on in our relationship. When I think back, I'm not sure why we were in such a hurry to plan a wedding so soon after he had proposed. There was no reason we couldn't delay or even move in together first. But excitement took over, and as happens with a fire sign such as me, when it does, things take their course real quick.

Because I had been in Greece a little less than two months prior and had discussed hypothetical wedding dates with my relatives (apparently, I was putting a wedding out into the Universe when I decided to have those conversations), it had been determined that the only way any of them could make it to my wedding was if it took place in the winter, as all their businesses were summer establishments that operated in the Crete tourist season between April 1 and October 31. Somehow, this led us to decide that January 7, a pretty big holiday in the Greek Orthodox tradition, would be the ideal date. Christmas Eve 2016 fell on a Saturday, New Year's Eve fell the following Saturday, and the Saturday after that would be our wedding day!

It seemed like an ideal scenario whereby anyone coming from Greece could do so throughout the holidays, enjoy those, and then enjoy our wedding next. That, though, led to me having to focus on so much more than I had initially intended for 2016, and I was having a hard time with the idea of compromising my business goals for the year. So I pushed myself ... and pushed myself some more.

By October 2016, I started freaking out that if we kept the wedding date for January 7, I would be putting myself at risk of falling into another depressive episode. How had this even entered my mind? My brother and my mother had expressed their concerns to my personal trainer about my being prone to depression, and that by having a lot going on with the certificate I was trying to complete, my private practice, planning the wedding, planning a move, and the trainer's pressure to turn me into Fergie by the wedding day, perhaps I would sink again.

I felt myself burning out, and since I knew there was still a window of opportunity where I could change the date without losing any money and messing things up for people who were planning to travel, I acquiesced to changing the date. I felt a lot of guilt because I knew that moving the date to spring would mean eliminating the possibility of close relatives from Greece attending our wedding. Though I was sad and worried about my family members, it was not a reason to put myself at risk of deepening my burnout and developing depression again. Little did I know that moving the wedding by less than four months was still insufficient time to preserve my sanity.

On January 8, 2017, I enjoyed an incredible bridal shower. My family surprised me, which I appreciated very much. I love surprises, whether I'm the one doing the surprise or the one getting surprised.

Subconsciously, my need for significance has likely been behind my need to be surprised and/or to surprise others. When certain core needs are not met at critical periods of our lives, typically from birth to age eight, those needs very often drive our decisions and actions throughout our adult lives. Unless we do the work and bring those unconscious needs to the forefront, they will continue to be what lies behind many of our emotions, actions, and direction in life. These needs are as much behind our bad decisions as they are behind the wonderful things we accomplish.

Bottom line, as a result of being the child of workaholic parents, some of my core needs were definitely not met, or not met enough, at least, and this has been behind a lot of my unhealthy behaviors.

We all prioritize our needs differently, and our decisions are based on which needs we put first. Once you learn to identify what those needs are and make conscious decisions about how to meet them, you can live a more aligned and healthy life, free of unnecessary suffering, such as anger, anxiety, and depression.

Don't get me wrong—I'm grateful my parents did everything they could to provide for us, and they modeled traits of persistence and determination that today are some of my best qualities. Work-life balance could have spared them so much grief, though, such as the wear and tear on their bodies and the emotional trauma they endured as a result of the major depressive episodes.

As a result of what I witnessed growing up, I adopted the art of pressuring myself. Clearly, I'd done a lot of that in 2016 and the first half of 2017 as I took on one major life transition after another, which is never a good idea, especially not for someone vulnerable to reexperiencing depression during periods of high stress. I thought I was done with depression, though, because I mistakenly believed that due to no longer having the learning difficulties I had struggled with most of my life, I was good to go.

Here's the thing—every life transition, however positive, is stressful! Yes, even adjusting to positive changes can cause stress, and the stress of change can be enough to induce mental health problems, such as anxiety and depression, for ANYONE, let alone someone with a history of depression. Stress actually drives us N.U.T.S.!

You read that correctly—N.U.T.S. is an acronym created by one of my McGill professors, Dr. Sonia Lupien, to explain the effects of stress in a nutshell. Essentially, the brain will release stress hormones if a situation is more than one of the following: **Novel, Unpredictable, Threatening** (either to your self-esteem or your ego), and something over which you don't have a **Sense of Control.** You don't have to work long hours or deal with life-and-death issues to feel stressed. It happens to us all for various reasons, especially during life transitions, given that all four sources of stress are usually present.

Part of loving yourself authentically entails examining the current stressors in your life, your unhealthy reactions to these stressors, and the unhealthy thought patterns that have taken over your brain. At the time, I didn't really love myself authentically, and as I have said time and time again on my livestreams and social media posts, a shortage of self-love nearly killed me more than once.

So here I was in the first couple months of 2017, looking for a new apartment, furniture shopping, moving out of my parent's home, and moving into an apartment with Mike while continuing to plan a big fat Greek wedding (it was more of a production, really), growing my private practice and my social media following on Instagram, planning a big honeymoon, taking classes, and still training for that "Fergie" body by my wedding.

All this during a harsh winter with little to no sunlight, while the EAP contracts consistently sent me clients suffering from depression. It's no secret that there is a difference in how much more taxing a session can be when a client comes to you with a diagnosis of depression versus coming to you for a workplace conflict they need to resolve. To say I was exhausted leading up to my wedding is an understatement. I had no idea that I had begun experiencing burnout during that time and that stress was silently killing me.

In North America, most people experiencing burnout push through it because running on fumes has unfortunately been normalized over the years, if not celebrated. To top it all off, as the 3:16 Day of 2017 approached, I was hard on myself for not being more prepared to take this project much further. I put more pressure on myself to figure out what I would do that day while already being overwhelmed with wedding-related details, keeping on top of the certification I was working toward, and catching up with client notes I had fallen behind on.

I reluctantly accepted that I couldn't yet grow this Movement to the desired level, given that it was crunch time for the wedding. I had difficulty seeing it. It took my brother noticing how exhausted I was the night before 3:16 Day of that year to tell me that I needed to pace myself regarding the Movement and that, in due time, the Movement would grow.

However, I was still trying to make it all work, almost as if I had forgotten what depression was like, even after making it a point to let the world know I had survived it, along with a suicide attempt. There was a disconnect between what I was saying and preaching. Six years had gone by, and that episode, along with 3:16 Day, seemed like a distant memory that didn't make me uneasy when I thought about it, almost as if it had never happened.

Tony and I created a short yet powerful video regarding why I post at 3:16 and why this day is important. I was so tired after we finished, yet I still wanted to post it the next day, knowing there would be notifications left and right, even phone calls, since a lot of people who knew me still had no idea I had attempted suicide six years prior.

Did I need to add one more thing to my plate that would require me to give so much energy in the following days? The Short and honest answer is NO. Was I oblivious to how bad things had gotten for my mental health by that point? The short and honest answer is YES.

So, on March 16, 2017, six years after surviving a suicide attempt, we released that one-minute video (now on www.join316.com). I didn't just make one post; I made FIVE posts that day to make sure as many people as possible would see it because I wouldn't be able to post or do much regarding this Movement that I was so eager to progress.

Everything I predicted happened. The notifications nearly blew up my phone, and I answered every single comment, text, and call.

Normalizing the conversation had officially reached another level, making my heart sing.

I lived off this high for a few days while in the grind of things. Then, exactly one month before the wedding, on March 29, I attended a Tony Robbins all-day event in Montreal. It was a "Power of Success" twelve-hour seminar featuring multiple successful speakers to elevate us and promote their programs. Tony Robbins spoke for even longer than expected and offered life-altering advice (some of which I was already aware of because the last certification I was working on at the time was part of the Robbins-Madanes Training he offers).

I left that event feeling even higher, and the next day, I brought a very different energy into my sessions. I was also pumped to achieve my entrepreneurial goals and looking forward to my wedding and honeymoon being over with! Imagine that—I had worked so hard planning everything, and even though the events hadn't happened yet, I was already on to the next thing in my mind. A classic case of not really enjoying a journey and instead anticipating the final destination. It's not helpful and not healthy either.

Still, I was finding ways to work on more things during crunch time since I was concerned about losing my momentum from the Robbins event, which was front row and up close and personal with Tony, someone I truly look up to.

Before I knew it, the week before my wedding had arrived, and only the close relatives who didn't run tourist season businesses had flown in. I took that week off to greet them and tie up loose ends for the wedding day. Clearly, it wasn't really a week "off," given all the running around I had to do, but I didn't want to take longer than a week before the wedding as our honeymoon was scheduled to last three weeks. Factoring that I would also need a couple of days to recover, I did not want to take more than five weeks off as I wouldn't say I liked the idea of leaving my clients hanging for so long.

I remember feeling really tired that week and even begging my mom—yes, begging her—to cancel the Thursday night pre-wedding event she had planned. I was going to pick up the musicians from the airport that day, and we could've just had dinner with them at the house since they would be sleeping there, anyway. But no, my entire family insisted that it was tradition and that everything would run smoothly, and I would take all day Friday to relax. My gut told me that wouldn't be enough, as clearly, my flame had started flickering long before that Thursday rolled around.

The Thursday night pre-wedding event happened, and yes, we had a really good time. I could barely sleep that night—from the excitement? From the hamster spinning on its wheel in my head? Was it a symptom of burnout? Most likely, all of the above.

That Friday before my wedding, I was beyond exhausted when I went for my manicure and pedicure, followed by some last-minute wedding details. On the morning of my wedding, while my favorite makeup artist did what she did best, I burst into tears. Someone had just said that Mike and the groomsmen were stuck in intense traffic as Montreal had begun mass construction across the island. The men running that late meant we would not take photos where I'd wanted to, and that little add-on of stress sent me over the edge.

Bridesmaids and my mom started coming in as they heard me crying, and my makeup artist told them I was emotional because of the day itself. I'm not sure to what extent she believed her own bullshit, but it was enough to get them out of the room so that I could stop crying and she could finish her artwork.

The wedding day didn't go off without a hitch, which was to be expected, given how many pieces there were to this production. The things that did go wrong were unexpected, and I felt very angry the next day and up until the day I boarded our flight to Dubai.

From an outsider's perspective, it was not only the wedding of the year but the wedding of the decade. That wasn't my perspective, though, as I had totally fixated on the things that were supposed to happen during my wedding that didn't, things that meant so much to me. I managed to start having a good time at my wedding at 1:45 a.m. when everything on the schedule for the evening had been completed, and I no longer had to think of anything; I could just relax.

In retrospect, I can say that I would have greatly benefitted from a wedding planner or at least a wedding coordinator that night. Since then, I've done nothing but recommend this to future brides, especially those who consider planning something of the magnitude of our wedding.

At 1:45 a.m., I went to the bar and ordered two Malibu and pineapple cocktails, the first time any alcohol entered my system that day. I literally chugged them one by one in front of the bartender and guests and then ran up on stage to dance with my husband to some Oriental beats that my best friend played on his drum.

This "stress-free" time lasted until about 4:30 a.m., and with the night officially over, we walked to the McDonald's across the street. My husband and I had reserved the wedding suite at the next-door hotel, so a little McDonald's run wouldn't delay us from sleeping. However, I didn't fall asleep until 7:00 a.m. and was wide awake by 7:45. This is how the first day of my marriage began—running on fumes.

We returned to the hall to tie up loose ends and carry on with other errands. Then, we gathered at my parents' home with all the other out-of-town guests and musicians who had flown in. Rest clearly continued to be off the menu.

In the next twenty-four hours, I ran around town and took care of post-wedding errands while packing for a nineteen-day honeymoon to two very different destinations in style and weather—Dubai and Bali. I found myself thinking about what had gone wrong at the wedding and crying throughout the day.

Eventually, I managed to pull myself together, and we even went to the airport to send off the musicians, which was really not necessary but just one more thing I had a hard time saying no to.

The next day, it was our turn to fly out, and I kid you not, the obsession over what had gone wrong at the wedding continued to be very present, leading me to leave Montreal on a terrible foot. I remember my mom and brother being really concerned about me but also angry with the person who'd contributed to my wedding disappointment. They weren't scolding me for appearing ungrateful about how well everything else had gone, but they were totally feeding off my anger and agreeing with my major complaints.

Luckily, after we boarded the plane, Mike chose a movie, and I put on the audio version of a mindfulness book I'd wanted to read. Over several hours, I found myself letting go and forgiving the person I had been infuriated with. I had Wi-Fi on the plane and made it a point to message my family to let them know I was way better than how I left them. I promised that we would have a fantastic time on our honeymoon.

And we did just that.

The first six days of our honeymoon were in Dubai, the latter nine in Bali, and then we returned to Dubai for one more night. Rest, which is what I needed most, continued to evade me. When we got to Dubai, I slept more than usual and at very odd hours, not having anything to do with the jet lag. I recall my relative who lives in Dubai pointing out how there was something odd about how much I was sleeping in those first few days and the hours I was waking up. I didn't care; I just wanted to sleep some more, but I felt guilty about Mike being unable to do some of the things he wanted us to do in Dubai.

That right there was another indication of my running low on self-love. Despite my exhaustion, I was very much preoccupied with meeting someone else's and my husband's needs. And unfortunately, this didn't end there.

I had been looking forward to spending ten hours a day on a Bali beach, not realizing that my husband couldn't stand being at the beach for more than an hour. He has hardcore ADHD, feels restless when staying in one place too long without stimulation, and has sensitive eyes to the sun. Who knew that I would marry someone who is the complete opposite of me when it comes to going to the beach—my happy place—?

On the first day, when Mike really wanted to go back to the room after an hour, I felt guilty for wanting to spend my days at the beach. I contacted one of my best friends in New York who had been to Bali on her honeymoon a few months before and recommended I hire a chauffeur to take us to all the wonderful sites Bali offers. And God knows there are many. I asked her for the name of the chauffeur she was pleased with and started making calls and plans so I could make sure Mike would have the best honeymoon ever.

Here's the thing: Mike never asked me to leave the beach early, nor did he complain about my wanting to go to the beach. He expressed that he was more than happy to return to the room and read some of the books he'd brought out of the sun and in a cooler environment. I am the one who made a bigger deal out of this than necessary, and I am the one who had a hard time establishing a compromise that would work for both of us. I was very much forgetting what would be best for me at this point, as I guess the much-needed vitamin D we'd been missing all winter had already started to boost my mood. Plus, getting a chauffeur for an entire day in Bali cost USD 50, which was too good to pass up.

The roads in Bali are a mess, so I hired Jefta, and for five days out of that trip, he took us everywhere on that magical island.

I even remember my relatives in Dubai, who had visited Bali a few times over the last twenty years, telling me that we had done and seen more during those nine days than they had in all their trips combined. You can imagine that meant I was NOT returning to Montreal any more rested than I'd left.

When we returned home, I was exhausted and physically unwell, as I had contracted Bali belly toward the end of our trip caused by consuming bacteria found in contaminated water. I had a lot of very uncomfortable cramping like nothing I'd ever experienced before. Readjusting to the Eastern Time zone also took its toll. This pushed back my return to the office by a couple more days, making me feel worse about the delay in resuming client appointments.

When I got to my office several days later, I sat at my desk, and something unusual happened. Whatever was on my desk, whatever files I had left incomplete the weeks before my wedding (and there were quite a few), whatever loose ends I needed to tie up on my return, all felt insurmountable. Then I opened my work emails and saw an overdue notice—more like a warning at this point, since I had not responded to the notice the week of my wedding—regarding the Order of Guidance Counsellors (whom I was licensed with) requesting to audit my files as part of an annual procedure they do to randomly selected members.

Right then, anxiety set in because I knew there was no way in hell I could prepare everything in time for an audit they were aiming to conduct in a few days.

I emailed them, in a panic, lying through my teeth about still being out of town, trying to buy myself time, and I started pushing through the anxiety at that moment. The next day, I resumed seeing clients, even while feeling very uneasy about my situation.

This went on for a few more days, and then on June 10, after completing a ninety-minute coaching session with a client, I noticed several missed calls from Mike and my mother-in-law. Already feeling tired and numb, I called Mike back, only for him to tell me that he'd been injured at work and had been at the hospital for the last hour and a half.

I froze. I didn't know what to do. He told me he was OK but that he sustained a nasty cut on his thumb and would likely need surgery, but they were unable to provide further details yet, and I needed to get over there as soon as I was done with work.

Mike and I went home that night and then experienced another eleven stressful days as he absolutely needed surgery, but there were no rooms available. A surgeon was available, but an operating room was not, so we were on standby for eleven days, unable to go too far from the hospital radius in case we got called in for his surgery. That was beyond frustrating, and I didn't have much bandwidth to allocate to more frustration. I stopped accepting new EAP referrals once I completed the sessions with other clients from those programs.

The surgery finally happened and ended up lasting three hours (instead of the promised thirty minutes) to repair what turned out to be a severed artery, tendon, and nerve. Waiting three hours for Mike to get out of surgery was very distressing, and it depleted me even more than I already was upon going into the hospital with him.

After Mike's discharge, he needed tending over the first few days. He also had difficulty sleeping in the position the doctor recommended and found himself moving around and waking me up a lot during the night. My sleep was pretty bad so that certainly didn't help. The audit was scheduled to happen soon, and I was nervous as hell. It had taken so much to achieve the equivalency requirements (from my education outside Quebec) to be able to get this license to practice, so the idea of losing it was very anxiety-provoking.

Every time my parents saw me, I was on edge. I didn't want to visit anymore as I was beyond tired after my sessions, most of which took place in the evenings, and I couldn't wait to get through the audit. It's as if I would only allow myself regular life activities after this potential audit was finished. I didn't care to talk to or see anyone else at that point, and even dealing with Mike, who was scared of never regaining the full function of his thumb, which would render him unable to move forward in his cooking career, had become too much.

Recovering from an injury or surgery that nearly cost someone their livelihood can be a challenging and emotional experience. Depending on the nature and severity of the surgery, one may have to face a long and difficult road to recovery, which may include physical pain, fatigue, and difficulty with everyday tasks. The added financial stress and uncertainty that comes with being unable to work during recovery surely doesn't help.

Mike experienced all of this at that point, and his mental and emotional well-being were undoubtedly affected. I noticed him feeling overwhelmed and distressed about his situation, and by that point, I also found myself more distressed, given that I would have to pay our steep rent on top of my office rent.

Mike was worried about how he would support us and when he would be able to do so again, and I was worried about how I would support us if the audit of my files went south. He was frustrated and discouraged by being unable to return to his normal routine, and I was frustrated beyond measure about our routines being disrupted. Nowhere in all this did I show empathy or understanding. I was so depleted and consumed by my struggles that I failed to show the love of my life that everything was going to be all right.

Someone in this predicament needs to have a strong support system, whether it's family, friends, or a support group, and to consider getting counseling or coaching to cope with the stress of the entire situation. Unfortunately for Mike at that point, the person he was living with wasn't the ideal support, as I wasn't patient nor a beacon of hope for him. It had become evident (and confusing to him) that I would provide a poor contribution to his recovery; I barely wanted to be around him, and he could tell.

Mike wasn't imagining things, as others, including my mom, had confirmed, noticing that I wasn't at my most pleasant around him or anyone. Honestly, I don't recall how I ended up agreeing to go for lunch with him just a few days before the audit. Still, I did, and we even ended up having a huge and unnecessary argument, asking for the check way sooner than we normally would. After this short and unpleasant lunch in Westmount, we coldly walked back to our apartment together. I rushed out of the elevator without him, and upon reaching our door, I had to slow down and dig deep into my purse for my keys. By the time I inserted the key into the keyhole, he had caught up to me, and as I turned the key to the right, Mike asked,

"Sophs...

Do you think you might be depressed?"

Epilogue

SELF-LOVE IS AN ONGOING conscious choice that each and every one of us <u>can</u> make, and that is absolutely worth making.

Why?

Because, as you now know, making the opposite choice nearly killed me.

A shortage of self-love is really what led to burnout. A shortage of self-love led me to push through that burnout and develop a brutal episode of major depression that led me to nearly end my life more than once.

By now, I hope you believe me when I tell you that ***Depression DOESN'T Discriminate***. This unseen *monster* can happen to any one of us, no matter how well life appears to be going.

The good news is that learning to love yourself can transform your life and save it.

I believe I'm still here because my purpose is to prevent as many people as possible from having to experience what I did, to prevent you from ever having to experience that, and to teach you how to love yourself as if your life depended on it. Because it does.

As I wrote this book, the project developed into something greater than I could have ever imagined!

Visit **www.join316.com/epilogue** to watch a short video about the experience of writing this book and learn what's coming up next in Part 2 of ***Mom, I Have a Problem.***

You will also receive a FREE Gratitude Guide to help you start building a daily habit of practicing and embodying gratitude for no more than 1% of your day!

Additionally, discover a list of my favorite books and other resources that have significantly contributed to my healing and emotional wealth journey, especially since I completed this book in late October 2022.

These invaluable resources are too precious to wait until the release of book 2 to share with you *because, as I've said time and time again, "Life is too short to be and feel anything else but alive."*

About the Author

Sophia Manarolis, M.Ed., emanates unapologetic authenticity, fearlessly embracing her humanity adorned with scars and vulnerability. Her commitment to speaking her truth isn't a mere declaration; it's a potent force that defines her. Beyond overcoming major depression and multiple suicide attempts, she proudly stands as a mental health warrior—a beacon of resilience.

With master's level counseling training and extensive life coaching training, Manarolis doesn't merely assist; she empowers clients to embrace a life that transcends mere existence, inviting them into an audacious dance of feeling lighter, freer, and vibrantly alive.

At the forefront of a global Movement, she isn't just a leader but a visionary on a mission—dedicated to eradicating unnecessary suffering that festers into burnout and depression. #its316andimalive isn't just a hashtag; it's her battle cry, reshaping the narrative surrounding depression and ensuring that those in silence recognize their strength to fight alongside her.

Born and raised in Montreal, Canada, to Greek parents who immigrated in the seventies, Sophia completed her primary and secondary education in French before pursuing a bachelor's degree in Psychology at McGill University. Subsequently, she attained her master's in counseling at the University of Ottawa. From volunteering between her degrees to officially becoming a mental health professional, Sophia has devoted herself to serving hundreds of individuals.

Through the **3:16 Movement** and global talks, her goal is to impact millions, if not billions! Currently residing on the enchanting island of Crete, Greece, with her wonderful husband Mike and three beloved cats—Erotokritos, Aretousa, and Socrates—Sophia's influence extends globally. Alongside her remarkable online services, she hosts **VIP Days** and short to medium **Bespoke Retreats** in Crete, with plans for longer transformative **Emotional Wealth Retreats**. For details on events in Crete, visit www.alive316.com.

Her mantra confidently proclaimed echoes: "Life is too short to be and feel anything else but ALIVE." It's not just a statement but a declaration conveying urgency—a call to fully embrace and experience life.

Sophia can be contacted via:

www.alive316.com

sophia@its316andimalive.com

Bonus

As you reach the end of this book, I'm thrilled to offer you an exclusive opportunity to work on your personal growth through the ***Prosper Through Emotional Wealth*** training program.

This carefully crafted program empowers individuals like yourself to lead emotionally wealthier lives. Picture yourself overcoming fears, improving relationships, experiencing heightened happiness, and mastering communication skills—all while replacing that inner critic with a more constructive and supportive inner dialogue. The program, consisting of 22 video lessons totaling 11 hours of enriching content and accompanied by an extensive workbook, serves as a comprehensive guide for you to **eliminate unnecessary suffering and prevent further instances of it!**

Consider the profound impact this program can have on your life as you take the next step toward your well-being. With this bonus, I'm pleased to extend a **20% OFF Gift** on the ***Prosper Through Emotional Wealth*** training program. Your investment not only benefits you but has the potential to break old generational patterns, preventing unnecessary suffering for both yourself and, if applicable, your children.

Having personally assisted hundreds of individuals with the tools offered in this program and having traveled the path of self-love myself, I can attest to its transformative power. This journey is not just about loving yourself during the program; it's about embarking on a lifelong journey of emotional wealth that extends far beyond its completion!

By purchasing this book, you've contributed to normalizing the conversation around depression and mental health. Now, seize the opportunity to enhance your well-being and that of your loved ones. Visit www.alive316.com, select this program, and use Promo Code GRATITUDE20 at checkout. Let's embark on this journey of prosperity together!

Thank you again for reading my book. If you found this journey helpful or impactful in any way, I would greatly appreciate it if you could take a moment to share your thoughts. Your testimonial can inspire others to read this book, share its message, and help me open people's eyes! Feel free to leave a review on Amazon or Goodreads.

I truly wish you a beautiful and healthy future filled with increased self-confidence, assertiveness, improved relationships, emotional mastery, resilience, and the profound understanding that emotional wealth is paramount. Without it, financial wealth becomes worthless. A future where you love yourself... ALIVE.

With immense gratitude,

Sophia

Made in the USA
Columbia, SC
22 April 2024

30826d88-9140-4085-8b89-305167b19532R01